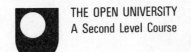
THE OPEN UNIVERSITY
A Second Level Course

The changing experience of women

Unit 1
The woman question

Prepared for the Course Team by
Veronica Beechey with Richard Allen

The Open University Press

U221 Course Team

Richard Allen
Francis Aprahamian (*Editor*)
Madeleine Arnot
Else Bartels
Veronica Beechey
Sylvia Bentley
Frances Berrigan (*BBC*)
Lynda Birke
Maria Burke
Ruth Carter
Barbara Crowther
Judy Ekins
Susan Himmelweit
Barbara Hodgson
Gill Kirkup
Diana Leonard
Vic Lockwood (*BBC*)
Judy Lown
Joan Mason
Perry Morley (*Editor*)
Rosemary O'Day
Fran Page (*Designer*)
Michael Philps (*BBC*)
Stella Pilsworth
Ann Pointon (*BBC*)
Sonja Ruehl
Mary Anne Speakman
Elizabeth Whitelegg

Consultants
Lesley Doyal (*Polytechnic of North London*)
Mary Ann Elston (*N.E. London Polytechnic*)
Catherine Hall (*Essex University*)
Jalna Hanmer (*Bradford University*)
Janice Winship

The Open University Press
Walton Hall, Milton Keynes
MK6 6AA

First published 1982; reprinted 1983, 1985

Copyright © 1982, 1983, 1985   The Open University

Designed by the Graphic Design Group of the Open University.

Typeset by Archway Press Ltd, Poole, Dorset BH15 2AF.

Printed in Great Britain by The Garden City Press Ltd, Letchworth, Hertfordshire SG6 1JS.

ISBN 0 335 10301 4

This text forms part of an Open University course. The complete list of Blocks in the course appears at the end of this text.

For general availability of supporting material referred to in this text, please write to Open University Educational Enterprises Limited, 12 Cofferidge Close, Stony Stratford, Milton Keynes MK11 1BY, Great Britain.

Further information on Open University courses may be obtained from the Admissions Office, The Open University, P.O. Box 48, Walton Hall, Milton Keynes MK7 6AB.

2.2

Contents

1	**Introduction and Study Guide**	5
2	**Women's autobiographies**	**6**
2.1	Mrs Wrigley	7
2.2	Virginia Woolf	10
2.3	May Hobbes	12
2.4	Micheline Wandor	15
2.5	Dr K. Tandon	18
2.6	Consideration of the extracts	20
2.7	Constructing an autobiography	21
2.8	Summary	21
3	**Women in newspapers**	**21**
3.1	A feminist analysis of the press	25
4	**Advertisements construct women**	**27**
4.1	Recent changes in advertisements	28
4.2	Ads construct their audience	30
4.3	Reversal	32
4.4	Summary	34
5	**Statistical quiz**	**35**
5.1	Public life	35
5.2	Employment	35
5.3	Education	36
5.4	Marriage, family and the household	36
5.5	A note about official statistics	37
5.6	Answers to the quiz	37
6	**Explanations of gender differences and inequalities**	**39**
6.1	Biologically determinist explanations	39
6.2	The liberal view	41
6.3	Analyses of women's oppression	43
6.3.1	Women's oppression located in power relations	43
6.3.3	Women's oppression related to the organization of production	45
6.3.3	Women's oppression rooted in biological differences	49
7	**Conclusion**	**51**
	References and further reading	**52**

1 Introduction and Study Guide

The aim of this Unit, *The Woman Question**, is to introduce you to some of the questions that have guided our thinking in devising the Course and to some of the themes which run through it. We have organized the text in a way which we hope will encourage and enable you to ask questions about the position of women. The Unit is divided into seven Sections. We start by considering the question of women's experience, which, as its title suggests, is a major concern of the Course. We approach the question of women's experience via three avenues in the first three Sections of the Unit.

In Section 2 we look at a series of autobiographical extracts written by women about themselves. We want you to think about how women write about themselves and about whether there are common themes running through these different extracts.

Section 3 considers how women's experiences are written about in daily newspapers. We look at what kinds of activities the newpapers report and at how they portray women on their pages.

Section 4 looks at how women are represented in advertisements, mainly in women's magazines. Here we want you to think about how women are represented visually as well as in written texts. Running through these three Sections are two questions that we would like you to keep in mind as you read the Unit. First, do women share common experiences as women, and how can we find out about these? Second, how are women depicted in autobiographies, the popular press and in the mass media?

Section 5 is a statistical quiz which looks briefly at some of the inequalities between women and men in contemporary British society — in public life, in employment, in the education system, and also in the family.

Section 6 is concerned with explanations. We consider some of the explanations that have been proposed to account for differences between women and men and for inequalities between the sexes. We focus particularly upon biological explanations, liberal explanations and a variety of feminist explanations, since these are the explanations you will encounter most often in the rest of the Course. Since theories seldom exist in a vacuum, and since many of the arguments presented in the Course have been put forward by people who are interested in the question of women's emancipation (however this is defined), we shall also consider in this final Section how different kinds of analysis imply different strategies for social change.

You should not be surprised not to find elaborated and final answers to the questions we ask in this Unit. Our aim is to map out some of the questions raised in the remainder of the Course, and to introduce you to some of the different ways of thinking about 'the woman question' rather than to provide you with answers. We hope that you will critically engage with the text throughout the Unit, questioning the assumptions on which the arguments are premised, asking alternative questions, and thinking about how your own experiences — whether as a woman or as a man — have been constructed.

This Unit represents two weeks of study time. In working through the Unit you should plan to spend about half your time on Sections 2–4 and half your time on Sections 5 and 6. Section 3 has an activity based on analysing a copy of a newspaper, any daily paper, which you should get hold of before you start†. We suggest you spend no more than two hours studying this Section and doing the activity. Section 5 is mainly a quiz, and you are not meant to spend a long time on it. We suggest an hour at the most. Section 6 is the most conceptually difficult one, so allow four or five hours for it. You might find it helpful to read this Section through once, and then to work through it more slowly, thinking about the theories and doing the activities.

You will find that the women in the first television programme (TV 1) bring up a lot of the issues raised in Section 2 of the Unit, and you should find it interesting to compare women speaking about themselves with the written autobiographical extracts in Section 2. There is no audiovisual component or set reading associated with this Unit.

*The term 'The Woman Question' was widely used in the nineteenth century.
†Keep this newspaper when you have finished this analysis, as you will need it later in the Course.

Women's autobiographies

In this Section we want you to read and think about some extracts from autobiographical writings by women. Feminists writing in recent years have often asserted that women's experiences have been 'hidden from history', that history books frequently provide an account of events that has excluded women, or has relegated them to the 'private' world of child-rearing and the family. Sheila Rowbotham wrote a book about women in history which she called *Hidden From History* to draw attention to the fact that women have been left out of historical accounts and yet have played an important role in the making of history. Autobiographical accounts seem to offer one obvious way in which to learn about the lives of women and how women have experienced the world. To a certain extent, then, they enable us to counteract the 'hiddenness' of women in orthodox accounts.

However, it should not be forgotten that autobiographical accounts tell only of the experience of particular individuals. A visit to a library or bookshop would suggest, too, that autobiographical writings by middle-class women have survived more and are more widely available than autobiographical writings by working-class women. This is partly because middle-class women have often had more education and more time and resources to enable them to write, and partly because of the policies of publishing houses. There has also been more of a tradition of middle-class women writing. The bulk of women's autobiographies in your local library is likely to have been written by women who have titles, or who are actresses or filmstars, or by women who have married men who have made them famous. The balance is being redressed somewhat by the policies of modern feminist publishers. Despite these initiatives, however, there is still far less autobiographical writing by workingclass women available, and even less by Afro-Caribbean and Asian women living in Britain.

We have tried in our extracts from autobiographical accounts to include extracts written by rather different kinds of women in different historical periods although, within the space available, our spectrum is still very narrow. We have selected the particular extracts because they contain themes which are prominent in the Course as whole, and because we think they are important. We do not, however, wish to imply that these women's accounts are in any way the most important autobiographies written by women, or the most typical. You should remember too that the different writers have constructed an account of their lives in a particular way; they have selected, consciously or unconsciously, the details to include.

The first two extracts were written in the same period, early in the twentieth century. The first, 'A Platelayer's Wife', written by Mrs Wrigley, is taken from a book of essays written by women in the Co-operative Women's Guild. This is called *Life as we have known it,* and was first published in 1931. Mrs Wrigley wrote her piece for the book in 1930, and in it reflected upon the previous seventy-two years of her life. The second extract is taken from the selection of Virginia Woolf's autobiographical writings, which were eventually published under the title *Moments of Being* in 1976. These pieces were written by Virgina Woolf as private memoirs between 1907 and the late 1930s.

The remaining extracts come from a later period, May Hobbes wrote an autobiographical book called *Born to Struggle* in 1973, after she had achieved some prominence through the London night-cleaners' campaign. The fourth piece was written by Micheline Wandor and is taken from a book of essays called *Why Children?,* which was published in 1980. Like Mrs Wrigley's 'A Platelayer's Wife', Micheline Wandor's essay is one of a series of autobiographical essays which were published as part of a collective project. The final extract is from an article called 'Lumps and bumps, racism and sexism', which appeared in the magazine *Spare Rib* in 1983. In it Dr K. Tandon writes about her experiences of training and working as a doctor.

● As you read through the extracts we would like you to think about the following questions:

1 What aspects of the woman's life seem most important in the extract?

2 What similarities and differences between the women's lives are suggested in the different extracts?

3 In so far as you find differences between the extracts, what do you think might account for these differences? Think, for instance, about how far differences of historical period seem to be important. And about the significance of social class and ethnic differences.

2.1 Mrs Wrigley

Life as we have known it, by Co-operative Working Women, contains five longer auto-biographical accounts and a number of shorter extracts taken, we are told, from a packet of papers gathered over the years by Margaret Llewelyn Davies, one of the founders of the Women's Co-operative Guild. Mrs Wrigley's account is one of the longer pieces published in this book. In the introductory letter to the volume addressed to Margaret Llewelyn Davies, Virginia Woolf makes the following comments:

> Sometimes, you said, you got a letter which you could not bring yourself to burn; once or twice a Guildswoman had at your suggestion written a few pages about her life. It might be that we should find these papers interesting; that if we read them the women would cease to be symbols and would become instead individuals. But they were very fragmentary and ungrammatical; they had been jotted down in the intervals of house work. Indeed you could not at once bring yourself to give them up, as if to expose them to other eyes were a breach of confidence. It might be that their crudity would only perplex, that the writing of people who do not know how to write — but at this point we burst in. In the first place, every English-woman knows how to write; in the second even if she does not she has only to take her own life for subject and write the truth about that and not fiction or poetry for our interest to be so keenly roused that — in short we cannot wait but must read the packet at once.
>
> (pp.xxxi – xxxii)

The book as a whole is a testimonial to the work of the Guild, particularly in giving a voice to 'the neglected needs of married working women . . .' (p.xiv), and to the achievements of its individual members in struggling for divorce, education and the vote, for higher wages and shorter working hours. Extract 1 describes Mrs Wrigley's childhood, her early married life and finally her work for the Guild.

Extract 1

I was born in Cefn Mawr (Wales), April 17th, 1858. My father was a shoemaker, and worked for his brother Jonathan Jones. He made the late Sir Watkin Williams Wynn's wellington boots. It was all hard work in those days. My father's earnings was 12s. per week, and there was five children. My mother went out day sewing for 1s. a day, when she could have work. I being the older one had to look after the other children. When mother was at home I had to go out and gather coal and cinders to make a fire, and walk two miles to a pit bank to pick coals, and carry it in a basket on my head. I also had to go two miles to a farm-house for buttermilk; we could have as much as we could carry for 2d., ten to twelve quarts it was mostly. Our food then was potatoes and bacon, red herrings and bread and milk. There was no such thing as tea for the children in those days. Clear water we had to carry on our heads from some spring well. I remember one time my mother had been out sewing all day from eight to eight, and I had gone to bed with the others, as my father said I could. But when mother came in there was no clean water for breakfast, so she made me get out of bed and go through a wood for some clean water. I am not saying what my other sister said, but she thought my mother very cruel. At that time I went out cleaning the floors and back-yards on a Saturday for a penny a time, and a piece of bread and butter. I also carried dinners and suppers to the iron forge for twopence a week.

Some of the happiest days of my childhood were when my mother packed us off with food for the day with other children, and to take the clothes to wash. Then, by the River Dee, we would take a bucket full of coal and get a few boulder stones and make a fire to boil the clothes in the bucket, and rinse them in the river, for there was plenty of water and we hadn't to carry it. Then, while the clothes was drying we had a good romp. We would take the babies with us as well, for there was plenty fields for them to pick the little daisies, and the older ones looked after the little ones. Some of our parents would come down to see if we was all right, and then we would fold the clothes and go home singing and rejoicing that we had had a good washing day and a good play.

All this was when I was about eight years old. When I was about nine, the Vicar of the Church asked if I would go to be with his children and take them out. There was another servant, but I did not stay long, for we were rationed with our

7

food and everything was locked up. My mother was glad for me to go out for food alone.

I had been at home a few days when the doctor's wife came to our house and said a lady and gentleman wanted a little nurse for their child, to go back with them to Hazel Grove, near Stockport. My little bundle of clothes was packed up and I went in full glee with them. Instead of being a nurse I had to be a servant-of-all-work, having to get up at six in the morning, turn a room out and get it ready for breakfast. My biggest trouble was I could not light the fire, and my master was very cross and would tell me to stand away, and give me a good box on my ears. That was my first experience of service life. I fretted very much for my home. Humble as it was, it was home. Not able to read or write, I could not let my parents know, until a kind old lady in the village wrote to my parents to fetch me home from the hardships I endured. I had no wages at this place, only a few clothes.

My next situation was on a farm where they kept 150 milking cows, near to Oswestry. It was there where I learnt to milk and make cheese and butter. I was very happy there looking after the calves, ducks, hens and chickens, and gathering the eggs. My wage was 2/6 per month. I stayed there until I was twelve years old. Then I went to another farm in Marple, where I was very comfortable and happy. My wages there was 3/- per month. I had five cows to milk morning and night, clean the shippens out, take the cows to the field and churn the butter in the afternoon, and four little children to look after while my mistress was busy in the shop. It was in the time of the great flood at Marple in 1871.

My third situation was in Oldham in 1872, at a Temperance Hotel. I was then fourteen years old. Seeing as I could not read or write, my master and mistress took an interest in me and paid for my education at the night school for two years. He also helped me at night with my lessons. They proved a father and mother to me. I was with them until I was nineteen years old, and I have a great deal to be thankful for in their kindness. They have passed away now, but I see their sons very often. My wage was 16/- per month, and was raised to 20/- per month before I left.

I had a little holiday at home, and got another place at Dobcross, Saddleworth, for a little more money. It was a big house and I worked very hard from morning till night. There was a big family and I did all the washing. I was not allowed out only on Sunday afternoon and one Sunday night a month. When a girl can go out and have a little freedom her work does not feel half the trouble to her. It was one Sunday afternoon at school I first saw my husband, and when my mistress got to know, she stopped me going out altogether. I wonder if the girls of to-day would stand that! I stayed with them two years until I was twenty-one, when I left for a better place.

Here there was four servants, and I was engaged for the cook. It was a real gentleman's house. They kept coachman, farmer and gardener, the very best place I had in all my life. We had plenty of freedom, going out in our turn. We were not treated as servants but as all one family, and the children was taught to treat us kindly and with respect. The servants was thought so much of, and when we had a ball the kitchen staff was allowed to have one dance with the guests. My master and mistress was real Christian and she was the kindest lady in the village. Everybody was alike to her, but she had her house rule kept in order. Not one of us was allowed out one minute after nine o'clock. The bell rang out " all in," but the girls loved her too much to disobey her. I was there five years, and married from there. I was sorry to give up such a good home, and they was sorry for me to leave, but my young man wanted to get married for he had no mother. I had a good send-off with many presents.

My husband was only a platelayer on the line and his wages was 18/- per week. Out of that he had 1/- for his pocket, and 1/- for tobacco, and 7d. for his Provident Club and pension, leaving me with 15/5 to carry on. Out of that I paid 2/8 rent, 1/4 for coal and lamp-oil, which cost 6d. then for three quarts, leaving me with 10/11 to live on for the week. I could not go out working, for I had never been in a mill. I did a little plain sewing to help us during the week to keep out of debt. We struggled along to get a nice home together, with my little sewing money. My first thing to do was to join the Co-operative Stores in one of the Oldham branches, and I am glad to say I have been a member for forty-six years. I cannot say how it has helped with my little children.

I had been married five months, when I found out my condition, and to prepare for that time, I took more sewing in, and worked night and day to save a little, working the machine and washing, anything to save a shilling or two. Just a week before my baby came, I made eight print tight-fitting jackets for 1/4 each, to get a little more to what I had saved. I had to suffer for it after. I went about with a little pillow under each arm for three months with gathered breasts. I had a very good neighbour, she helped me all she could, but mother had to come to take me home to get better. While I was away, my husband was taken ill, and I nearly lost him. I am glad to think women are better looked after in these days.

I remember one of my old neighbours. She was in a very poor way, hadn't much to live on, her husband being a gasser in a mill, and had 18/- per week. There was five children to keep and her rent 4/- per week. Day after day she went out washing and cleaning and taking washing in. Sometimes she run into debt for groceries, and her husband got very cross with her. She told me herself that she had gone without many a meal for the children and her husband, still he worried her for going into debt. She could not pledge, for there was nothing to pledge; it was a poor home. Her husband was a steady man, but the same as other men—went out and left her to it to do as she liked. She could not sew or mend for the children as she would like, and they had to go with very little on their backs. She went cleaning for two ladies that lived not far from here. These ladies went away for the summer months, and left her in charge of the house to put fires in. In a lumber-room there was a marble timepiece. She did not know what to do for the next meal. She took the timepiece and pledged it for a few shillings, with the intention to take it back before they came home. But the ladies returned sooner than was expected. They missed the timepiece and wanted to know where it had gone to. She told them all about it and how sorry she was to have to do such a thing. The ladies gave her so many hours to bring it. Her husband knew nothing about it, and at ten o'clock that night she was locked up all night and her five children in bed. Her husband could do nothing till next day. His master lent him money to pay the cost. The neighbours turned against her, and I felt so sorry for her I took them some food in as she was fretting very much. In a few days she sent for me and there was the baby born, and only a little boy in the house. I sent for the nurse, and I took some bed-clothes, made her bed, and looked after her until she was well, and washed her clothes.

She has never forgotten what I did for her. The baby is a fine young man twenty-two years of age. ...

Had it not been that I took an interest in public work, I could not have stood it. There was the Women's Co-operative Guild, to which I owe a great deal for my education. I have been a member from the beginning of our Branch, a worker on Committees, and President for two years. We are glad to think that we in the Guild have taken our place in the fight for better conditions for women and children.

I joined the Suffrage, because having had such a hard and difficult life myself, I thought I would do all I could to relieve the sufferings of others. I took great interest in all women's organisations. When the war broke out, I helped on the Relief Committees all through the war. Miss Wilkinson (now M.P.) was one of the first to open a work-room in Stockport, to find work for girls in making old clothes for new for the poor children. We went round begging old cast-offs, and good work was done. Miss Wilkinson helped towards getting the Maternity Centre formed in Stockport. When investigating cases for relief we came across many pitiful homes where father had gone to the war, and four or five children had to be fed. I don't think we should have had war if the women could have had the vote before, and a voice in it. There's no mother or wife in England nor Germany that would give their loved one to be killed. Now we are working for peace. (pp. 56-65)

● Now that you have read the extract, pause for a moment and make a note of what this particular extract suggests are the key areas of Mrs Wrigley's life.

Looking after her younger brothers and sisters, working as a servant, marriage and pregnancy, struggling to make ends meet and political work for the Co-operative Women's Guild and the Suffrage, seem to us to be the most important areas reflected in the extracts. As a young girl Mrs Wrigley, then Miss Jones, had to look after her younger brothers and sisters and to do a share of the housework — at least in part, so that her mother could earn enough money to help support the family. Before marriage, like many young working-class women in the Victorian and Edwardian periods, she worked as a servant in other people's homes.

When Mrs Wrigley married and had a family of her own, she managed by taking in sewing because her husband's wages were low. She describes 'working day and night to save a little, working the machine and washing, anything to save a shilling or two' (p.61). Her neighbour too took washing into her home, as well as going out washing and cleaning. Mrs Wrigley eventually had five children, all boys, who were apprenticed to different trades. Despite her busy life, she still found time to help others. Mrs Wrigley tells us how she helped her neighbour and describes her involvement in the Women's Co-operative Guild, to which she owed her education. Through this, she got involved in public life, fighting for better conditions for women and children, and working on Relief Committees during the First World War.

9

2.2 Virginia Woolf

Life as we have known it appeared originally with an introductory letter by Virginia Woolf. At the end of this letter she describes women like Mrs Wrigley as 'voices . . . beginning only to emerge from silence into half articulate speech' (p.xxxxi). Much of the letter is taken up with a reflection on the contradictory and complex feelings that beset Virginia Woolf when she attended a Congress of the Women's Co-operative Guild in 1913:

> All these questions . . . which matter so intensely to the people here, questions of sanitation and education and wages, this demand for an extra shilling, for another year at school, for 8 hours instead of 9 behind a counter or in a mill, leave me, in blood and bones, untouched. If every reform they demand was granted this very instant it would not touch one hair of my comfortable capitalistic head. Hence my interest is merely altruistic . . . However hard I clap my hands or stamp my feet there is a hollowness in the sound which betrays me. I am a benevolent spectator. I am irretrievably cut off from the actions. I sit here hypocritically clapping and stamping an outcast from the flock.
>
> . . . if it were possible to meet them not as masters or mistresses or customers with a counter between us, but over the wash-tub or in the parlour casually and congenially as fellow-beings with the same wishes and ends in view, a great liberation would follow, and perhaps friendship and sympathy would supervene . . .'
>
> . . . But, we said, and here perhaps fiddled with a paper knife, or poked the fire impatiently by way of expressing our discontent, what is the use of it all? Our sympathy is fictitious, not real. Because the baker calls and we pay our bills with cheques, and our clothes are washed for us and we do not know the liver from the lights we are condemned to remain forever shut up in the countries of the middle classes . . . And they remain equally deprived. For we have as much to give them as they to give us. . . But the barrier is impassable. (pp.xx-xxx)

● Pause for a moment and think about what these paragraphs suggest is the most important cause of difference between Virginia Woolf and the women from the Women's Co-operative Guild.

You might think that an important cause of difference is social class. Virginia Woolf was born Virginia Stephen. Her own family was upper middle-class and relatively prosperous. Their life style was quite different from the typical Guildswoman. Money was not limitless in the Stephen household and, since a good deal of the family's income came from investments and legacies, the keynote was prudent budgeting rather than extravagant consumption. Virginia's father, Sir Leslie Stephen, was one of the leading intellectuals of the Victorian era, author of a number of prestigious books and editor of the *Dictionary of National Biography*. He was also essentially a Victorian patriarch. He married twice, and Virginia was one of the three children of the second marriage. Her mother, Julia Duckworth, had a daughter and two sons by a previous marriage. Virginia recorded her life in a diary which she kept for long periods of her life and she also wrote a number of autobiographical essays. Extract 2 comes from an essay, 'A Sketch of the Past', written in 1939–40, but not published until long after her death. The essay takes the form of a diary of remembrances of the past, written in the shadow of the oncoming war. Here she describes her family life around 1900 (roughly contemporary with the second extract from Mrs Wrigley you have already read).

Extract 2

In 22 Hyde Park Gate round about 1900 there was to be found a complete model of Victorian society. If I had the power to lift out a month of life as we lived it about 1900 I could extract a section of Victorian life, like one of those cases with glass covers in which one is shown ants or bees going about their affairs. Our day would begin with family breakfast at 8.30. Adrian bolted his; and whichever of us, Vanessa or myself, was down, would see him off. Standing at the front door we would wave a hand till he disappeared round the Martins' bulging wall. This was a relic left us by Stella—a flutter of the dead hand which lay beneath the surface of family life. Father would eat his breakfast sighing and snorting. If no letters, "Everyone has forgotten me", he would groan. A long envelope from Barkers would mean of course a sudden roar. George and Gerald came down. Vanessa disappeared behind the curtain. Dinner ordered, she would dash for the red bus to take her to the Academy. If Gerald coincided, he would give her a lift in his daily hansom —the same hansom, generally; the cabman in summer wore a carnation. George having breakfasted more deliberately—sometimes he would persuade me to sit on, on the three-cornered chair, and tell me gossip from last night's party—he too would button on his frock coat and give his top hat a promise with the velvet glove and disappear—smart and debonair, in his ribbed socks and very small well polished shoes, to the Treasury. Left alone in the great house, with Father shut in his study at the top, the housemaid polishing brass rods, Shag asleep on his mat, and some maid doing bedrooms while Sophie I suppose took in joints and milk from tradespeople at the back door, I mounted to my room and spread my Liddell and Scott upon my table and sat down to make out Euripides or Sophocles for my bi-weekly lesson with Janet Case.

From ten to one we escaped the pressure of Victorian society. Vanessa, I suppose, under the eye of Val Prinsep or Ouless or occasionally Sargent, painted from the life—she would bring home now and then very careful pencil drawings of Hermes perhaps, and spray them with fixative; or an oil head of a very histrionic looking male nude. And for the same three hours I would be reading perhaps Plato's *Republic*, or spelling out a Greek chorus. Our minds would escape to the world which on this November morning of 1940 she inhabits at Charleston and I in my garden room at Monks House. Our clothes would not be much different. She wore a blue painting smock; I perhaps a blouse and skirt. If our skirts were longer, that would be the only difference. Forty years ago she was rather tidier, rather better dressed than I. The change would come in the afternoon. About 4.30 Victorian society exerted its pressure. Then we must be 'in'. For at 5 father must be given his tea. And we must be better dressed and tidier, for Mrs Green was coming; Mrs H. Ward was coming; or Florence Bishop; or C. B. Clarke; or . . . We would have to sit at that table, either she or I, decently dressed, having nothing better to do, ready to talk. . .

We both learned the rules of the Victorian game of manners so thoroughly that we have never forgotten them. We still play the game. It is useful; it has its beauty, for it is founded upon restraint, sympathy, unselfishness—all civilised qualities. It is helpful in making something seemly and human out of raw odds and ends. But the Victorian manner is perhaps—I am not sure—a disadvantage in writing. When I re-read my old *Common Reader* articles I detect it there. I lay the blame for their suavity, their politeness, their sidelong approach, to my tea-table training. I see myself handing plates of buns to shy young men and asking them, not directly and simply about their poems and their novels, but whether they like cream as well as sugar. On the other hand, this surface manner allows one to say a great many things which would be inaudible if one marched straight up and spoke out. It was when the lights went up in the evening that society came into force. During daylight one could wear overalls; work. There was the Academy for Nessa; my Liddell and Scott and the Greek choruses for me. But in the evening society had it all its own way. At 7.30 we went upstairs to dress. However cold or foggy it might be, we slipped off our day clothes and stood shivering in front of washing basins. Neck and arms had to be scrubbed, for we had to come into the drawing room at 8 o'clock in evening dress: arms and neck bare. Dress and hairdoing became far more important than pictures and Greek. I would stand in front of George's Chippendale glass trying to make myself not only tidy but presentable. On an allowance of fifty pounds it was difficult, even for the skilful, to be well dressed of an evening. For though a house dress could be made by Jane Bride, at a cost of a pound or two, a party dress cost perhaps fifteen guineas if made by Mrs Young. The house dress therefore might be, as on this particular night, made of a green stuff bought erratically at a furniture shop—Story's—because it was cheaper than dress stuff; also more adventurous. Down I came: in my green evening dress; all the lights were up in the drawing room; and there was George, in his black tie and evening jacket, in the chair by the fire. He fixed on me that extraordinary observant [illegible] gaze with which he always inspected clothes. He looked me up and down as if [I] were a horse turned into the ring. Then the sullen look came over him; a look in which one traced not merely aesthetic disapproval; but something that went deeper; morally, socially, he scented some kind of insurrection; of defiance of social standards. I was condemned from many more points of view than I can analyse as I stood there, conscious of those criticisms; and conscious too of fear, of shame and of despair— "Go and tear it up", he said at last, in that curiously rasping and peevish voice which expressed his serious displeasure at this infringement of a code that meant more to him than he would admit. (pp.127–30)

The family was, for Virginia Woolf, 'a complete model of Victorian society'. She makes it plain that middle-class family life — with its strict rules of etiquette and its emphasis upon appearances – restricted women. Virginia Woolf believed that women were oppressed by men. Her father insisted on family tea at five, her stepbrothers insisted on their right to an arrogant appraisal of Virginia and her sister. Looking back, Virginia feels that the conventions of middle-class Victorian family life had penetrated deeply into her character. She feels, for example, that the critical writings later collected in the *Common Reader* are marked by 'tea-table' politeness. The middle-class Victorian family also offered some space for Virginia: 'from ten to one we escaped', Vanessa to art school, Virginia to the study of language and literature. It was the family's belief that every individual had a right and a duty to better themselves through education and self-improvement, which gave Virginia some room for independence and pleasure.

Virginia Woolf

Earlier in 'A Sketch of the Past' Virginia describes further how her personality and her experience have been affected by men, who appear to affect her conception of her self, albeit unconsciously. As you read Extract 3, think about what can be learned from it about Virginia Woolf's sense of herself:

Extract 3

There was a small looking-glass in the hall at Talland House. It had, I remember, a ledge with a brush on it. By standing on tiptoe I could see my face in the glass. When I was six or seven perhaps, I got into the habit of looking at my face in the glass. But I only did this if I was sure that I was alone. I was ashamed of it. A strong feeling of guilt seemed naturally attached to it. But why was this so? One obvious reason occurs to me—Vanessa and I were both what was called tomboys; that is, we played cricket, scrambled over rocks, climbed trees, were said not to care for clothes and so on. Perhaps therefore to have been found looking in the glass would have been against our tomboy code. But I think that my feeling of shame went a great deal deeper. I am almost inclined to drag in my grandfather—Sir James, who once smoked a cigar, liked it, and so threw away his cigar and never smoked another. I am almost inclined to think that I inherited a streak of the puritan, of the Clapham Sect.

At any rate, the looking-glass shame has lasted all my life, long after the tomboy phase was over. I cannot now powder my nose in public. Everything to do with dress—to be fitted, to come into a room wearing a new dress—still frightens me; at least makes me shy, self-conscious, uncomfortable. "Oh to be able to run, like Julian Morrell, all over the garden in a new dress", I thought not many years ago at Garsington; when Julian undid a parcel and put on a new dress and scampered round and round like a hare. Yet femininity was very strong in our family. We were famous for our beauty—my mother's beauty, Stella's beauty, gave me as early as I can remember, pride and pleasure. What then gave me this feeling of shame, unless it were that I inherited some opposite instinct? My father was spartan, ascetic, puritanical. He had I think no feeling for pictures; no ear for music; no sense of the sound of words. This leads me to think that my—I would say 'our' if I knew enough about

Vanessa, Thoby and Adrian—but how little we know even about brothers and sisters—this leads me to think that my natural love for beauty was checked by some ancestral dread. Yet this did not prevent me from feeling ecstasies and raptures spontaneously and intensely and without any shame or the least sense of guilt, so long as they were disconnected with my own body. I thus detect another element in the shame which I had in being caught looking at myself in the glass in the hall. I must have been ashamed or afraid of my own body. Another memory, also of the hall, may help to explain this. There was a slab outside the dining room door for standing dishes upon. Once when I was very small Gerald Duckworth lifted me onto this, and as I sat there he began to explore my body. I can remember the feel of his hand going under my clothes; going firmly and steadily lower and lower. I remember how I hoped that he would stop; how I stiffened and wriggled as his hand approached my private parts. But it did not stop. His hand explored my private parts too. I remember resenting, disliking it—what is the word for so dumb and mixed a feeling? It must have been strong, since I still recall it. This seems to show that a feeling about certain parts of the body; how they must not be touched; how it is wrong to allow them to be touched; must be instinctive. It proves that Virginia Stephen was not born on the 25th January 1882, but was born many thousands of years ago; and had from the very first to encounter instincts already acquired by thousands of ancestresses in the past.

And this throws light not merely on my own case, but upon the problem that I touched on the first page; why it is so difficult to give any account of the person to whom things happen. The person is evidently immensely complicated. Witness the incident of the looking-glass. Though I have done my best to explain why I was ashamed of looking at my own face I have only been able to discover some possible reasons; there may be others; I do not suppose that I have got at the truth; yet this is a simple incident; and it happened to me personally; and I have no motive for lying about it. In spite of all this, people write what they call 'lives' of other people; that is, they collect a number of events, and leave the person to whom it happened unknown. Let me add a dream; for it may refer to the incident of the looking-glass. I dreamt that I was looking in a glass when a horrible face—the face of an animal—suddenly showed over my shoulder. I cannot be sure if this was a dream, or if it happened. Was I looking in the glass one day when something in the background moved, and seemed to me alive? I cannot be sure. But I have always remembered the other face in the glass, whether it was a dream or a fact, and that it frightened me.

These then are some of my first memories. But of course as an account of my life they are misleading, because the things one does not remember are as important; perhaps they are more important. (pp.67–9)

The memoir was never completed, perhaps becaused it seemed still too personal for publication. Its being written at all probably owes a good deal to Virginia's increasing and more public commitment to feminism. The passage reveals her sense of uncertainty about her appearance and her intense inhibitions about her own body. She relates these to the culture and attitudes of her father's family, which led her to feel shameful of her appearance, and to the advances of the step brother (the incident described here is not unique). Virginia also cautions the reader about accepting her reflections as valid. You may have noticed her own caveats in the final paragraphs when she says, 'Though I have done my best to explain why I was ashamed of looking at my own face I have only been able to discover some possible reasons; there may be others'... These then are some of my first memories. But of course as an account of my life they are misleading, because the things one does not remember are as important; perhaps they are more important.'

● We have already suggested that differences of social class may be important in explaining some of the differences between the lives of Virginia Woolf and Mrs Wrigley. Before you go on to read the next set of extracts, stop for a minute and make a note of the ways in which Mrs Wrigley's and Virginia Woolf's lives are different and of any similarities between the two women suggested by the extracts.

2.3 May Hobbes

The extracts in this Section are taken from May Hobbes' autobiography, *Born to Struggle*. In it she describes her life in a working-class community in the East End of London just after the 1939-45 war. Extract 4 is taken from a chapter called 'Work and Marriage'. Jenny who appears in it, was May Hobbes's stepmother. As you read through the extract, think about how May Hobbes's experiences of family life, of men and of employment compare with Mrs Wrigley's and Virginia Woolf's accounts. Think also about what May Hobbes feels needs to be changed for the lives of women to be improved.

Extract 4

I still think the week-end is a great time in anyone's life at the age of sixteen. The start of the weekend was the time when you had a few bob in your pocket and you felt great. There was Friday night and all Saturday and Sunday ahead of you. On Saturday night I would meet Jean at the café or call for her at her house on the other side of the square. Then we went on into London to the Lyceum. Our trick there was to make out we were waiting for someone who hadn't shown up, and stand around looking all forlorn. Nine times out of ten a couple of Yanks would come along and chat you up. 'Well,' we would tell them, 'it don't look as though the people we were going to meet are coming.' So they always said, 'Well, come on in with us.' Which, of course, we did. Then, as soon we were inside, we would lose them. It never failed.

It was usually about eleven when we came out of the Lyceum, and sometimes we would then go down to the Black and White café next to Liverpool Street Station, unless we knew there was a party going either at Jenny's or someone else's house. On Sundays I reckoned to sleep until about two o'clock, when I got up to have dinner, and then would either go with Jenny to visit Peter's grave, or else join up with Jean to go to the Old Vic, as our local fleapit was called. There we would meet our mates and the local blokes, and when that turned out we went up to the Carlton Café, which was the meeting-place for everybody on Sunday nights. On Sunday, though, Jenny always insisted I must be home by eleven, it being work the next day...

By now it was just before Christmas, and we decided to have the wedding in March. Looking back, I suppose we rushed into things too quick. Also I think we were pulled together through our troubled backgrounds. He had had a rotten life with his father away in a mental home, where he had been for years. His mother had had to go out to work, he and his sister had more or less fetched themselves up. It was like the old saying: 'Two of a feather cling together.'

It was not going to be a big white wedding, I told Jenny, but would be in the local registry office.

Jenny thought for a moment and asked, 'Is it because you might be pregnant, because you don't have to get married just for that. One more in the household won't make much difference.'

That was the great thing about Jenny. You would never be frightened to confide in her about anything. It wasn't the reason, I assured her. I wasn't having any baby.

Christmas had always been a great time at Jenny's, and this Christmas George spent with us as by now he was almost part of the family. Jenny always insisted on a family Christmas in our own home with everyone all together. 'I might not be here next Christmas,' she would say. On Christmas Eve we went round to the pub for a good old knees-up with everyone getting right drunk and having a go on the mike. I did my Johnnie Ray bit, as he was my idol at the time. I had all his records and every time he was in England I went to hear him. Then it was home from the pub for a great old ding-dong which carried over into the following morning. I do not think Jenny ever went to bed on Christmas Eve. On Christmas Day we would have our dinner and then sleep till the pubs opened up again. I would never go away from home for Christmas. ...

I suppose I should have seen then that the marriage was not going to work out, but I do not think I really knew what I wanted out of life. Like a lot of teenagers, I just thought marriage would mean independence and a life of roses and stars, not a rude awakening.

We broke for the moment, but after a fortnight he came round one night to say he had found a flat and that he would take it whether we got married or not. It was in Stoke Newington, so I agreed to go and look. The rent was fair enough, and it had two rooms and a bathroom. The landlady had taken a liking to George, thinking he was a Jewish boy. She was quite disappointed when she found he wasn't, but the wedding was on again.

In fact it was on and off like a yo-yo right up till the day before, and the wedding when it came was a laugh in itself. I had bought a 2s. ring from Woolworth's, and when we arrived at the registry office, there was my brother standing there and shining it up on his jacket sleeve. Within half an hour I lost the marriage certificate, and at our so-called reception and the party which followed I got so drunk I can remember almost nothing about what happened. George, though, never drank, and so he stayed cold sober. Things finished up that night with him sleeping at his mum's and me being taken back to Jenny's.

The next morning Jenny was crying all over the place and saying, 'If anything goes wrong, come back here,' and I was saying, 'I think I've done the wrong thing,' but somehow George and I got together again and decided to go to the flat. We started our married life with him out of work and me having to give up work at Horniman's because of their company rule. I managed to find a job packing at a Christmas card factory in Old Street. Sometimes, I remember, I had to walk there and back from Stoke Newington as I did not have the bus fare, and then I would worry about how I was going to buy something to eat in the evening. Usually the worry was unfounded as George mostly managed to get some money from somewhere during the day. One typical evening was when I had been thinking it was about time he had a job and had gone home that night all ready for a row. When I got in, however, he was nowhere around, but the cupboard had been filled and there was a box of fifty fags and a pound note on the table with a note saying:

'Had to go off somewhere else. Go to the pictures or bingo. See you later.'..

Eventually I brought Tony home and settled down to a chaotic life of looking after him. When he was about three months old we had yet another move to Linton Street just off New North Road – a couple of rooms, and for that, even in those days, we had to pay £6 a week as we had a child. Anyway, George was working straight at the time – he thought he had better in view of the child – though the only job he could get was labouring in a mason's yard where they made gravestones. The wages they paid were about £16 a week, and I could not work because of Tony.

Things were pretty hard once we had paid £6 rent a week, and Tony had to have special things bought for him as he was still very small. By Monday we were always skint. We were beginning to argue more and more, so I decided I had better get back to work. At the clinic I asked if I could get Tony into a nursery, but they told me that in their opinion he was too young, besides which, no places were vacant: I would just have to try and manage on the money my husband gave me. So I watched the notice boards for a baby minder. When I found one she seemed a nice enough woman, so I decided to let Tony go to her. Her charge was £1 10s. a week, which I thought quite fair, so I got a job to start on the Monday. When I told George, he hated the idea, but then he relented, saying, 'That's the only way we are going to survive.' He didn't know, he said, why I wouldn't let him go back and work the other way, as we always had a fair standard of living then.

Anyway, I started this job – in a watch factory. The money was not bad and the hours were nine till five. The job was sitting there sorting out all the watches returned with something wrong with them. It was quite a boring procedure. I kept going for about three months, then noticed Tony was more miserable than usual, so thought I would come home one dinner-time to collect him and take him to the clinic. I went to fetch him, and when I got to the house I could hear him crying. The woman let me in and he was lying in his pram the same as when I took him in that morning. What gave me the needle was that he was still in the same nappy he had had on at 8.30, and there was a red mark on his arm. He had knocked it against the pram, the woman said, but it looked to me as if he had been hit. So I told her he would not be back with her any more. I packed up work there and then, and when I told George that night I do not think he was sorry.

Soon we found ourselves getting into a worse state than before, and George packed in his straight job and went back to the other work with his brother-in-law. (pp.39-48)

In Extract 4 we see May going out with her friend, Jean, on a Saturday night. In it May also talks about marriage. Like many other teenagers, she thought of marriage as 'independence and a life of roses and stars'. It became, however, a 'rude awakening'. For May, being married did not mean that she didn't have a job. Her family was poor, and she worried about how they would eat. It seemed to be self-evident that she would work since her husband's wages were low and he was in and out of employment. Yet, being a paid worker fitted uneasily with being a mother. May writes of the difficulties of combining responsibilities for earning a wage with looking after her son, Tony. And the work available was low paid and routine — packing Christmas cards and sorting out watches.

● May Hobbes is, like Mrs Wrigley, a working-class woman. Yet she is writing about working-class life in a period nearly half a century after Mrs Wrigley. Before you go on to read Extract 5 from *Born to Struggle*, make a note of the ways in which May Hobbes's and Mrs Wrigley's lives appear to be similar from the extracts, and of the ways in which you think they are different.

May Hobbes later became involved in campaigning to improve women's working conditions. In Extract 5 she talks about her involvement in the London night-cleaners' campaign, which was organized to get cleaners into a union and to improve their pay.

Extract 5

One woman had been working fourteen solid years when she was made redundant. She could have another job, they said. Except it was miles from where she lived and impossible for her because of the fares and her family commitments, as they well knew. But by offering her another job they managed to side-step their obligation to give her redundancy pay. This is typical of the way they treat their workers.

After the work at the college stopped I applied for another post as supervisor. By now my photograph and bits about what I was up to had begun appearing in the papers. When I met the area supervisor to look at where I would be in charge, she recognized me at once. As soon as she started to say what a good thing the union was for the cleaners I felt suspicious. She had sacked me inside three days. The old supervisor wanted her job back, she said. O.K., I said, I would stay on as a cleaner in that case, seeing how she was short-staffed. Oh no, she did not think that would be appropriate, after having been a supervisor. I knew what she meant: the pressure was on and I was already blacklisted.

From that moment going around and organizing the cleaners became a full-time job for me, especially the night cleaners, who to my mind were the worst exploited. I enlisted the help of anybody who would be willing to give up an hour of their time once a week to go around the office blocks and start talking to the cleaners themselves. We formed ourselves into the Cleaners Action Group and printed leaflets saying that all cleaners should join the union, while at the same time pointing out they could not expect big increases overnight and would have to do their bit to keep the union on its toes. Otherwise the union would just accept their dues and leave it at that.

In our first two months it was amazing the way people rallied to help. It was a new thing to them. People had not realized the way women were working all through the night to keep life turning over for others. We got quite a few buildings organized as union labour, and as soon as the contractors woke up to the fact that it was not only some five-minute wonder in came the strong-arm gang.

They would send in their managers to issue warnings that if it was found any woman had joined a union it would mean her instant dismissal. At the time my old mate Brenda was night cleaning at the Canadian Embassy in Trafalgar Square.

She comes across one of our leaflets there, and sees it has on it my name and address. 'Oh yes,' she says, 'I know May. We worked together on an office block. She's my friend,' she says, and is telling the other women how it is quite right that they ought to join the union just as the manager stalks in. He gives her the sack there and then, and when she asks him why, he says he is not having any of his schemes messed up by the union.

One Saturday afternoon the manager of one of the big contractors tried to get me on the phone, only it was Chris who answered. He had got himself drunk, said Chris, to give himself the guts to do it. You could tell he was drunk by the way he spoke. What he had phoned to say, he said, was that if I did not lay off he would break my arms and legs and stuff my leaflets down my throat.

'O.K.,' said Chris, 'we'll meet you, because it will take someone bigger than a slag that is drunk to do it.'

'She's getting into something bigger than she thinks,' said the bloke, and I knew what he meant knowing the bandits involved in that business.

So, we told him, that was why we were carrying on with it until we had exposed his people and all the corruption in the getting of government contracts and won a fair deal for those that did the work.

Life got busy from then on. I started to get letters asking me to go and speak at meetings or to university groups. Then we were going out one night a week with two of us to a building and we were starting to get the area well covered. The main area of concentration for office cleaners was in the big blocks in the City of London. The contractors find it more profitable to make it night work, because then the type of person they get to do it is someone who needs the money for such luxuries in life as rent and food for their family and who is hence in a poor bargaining position.

The first building to become unionized had been the Board of Trade building, Sanctuary House. The women there were getting £12.50 for a forty-hour week. Then Companies House and Shell-mex House at Waterloo were also unionized. The Sanctuary House cleaners elected their shop steward and deputy shop steward, and the two of them were sacked at once on some flimsy excuse. So we had our first major strike, with Companies House coming out in support.

It was a good strike. For the first time the cleaners saw how they could get something done through solidarity. Jean Wright, the supervisor, came out with the women, which was unusual. Then we had the support of Women's Lib and the Socialist Women, among others, and many stuck with us all night on the picket line, where we enjoyed ourselves. The cleaners also saw that other people were concerned about them once they knew something about the situation. (pp.79–80)

2.4 Micheline Wandor

The following extracts are taken from Micheline Wandor's contribution to a book called *Why Children?* The book contains accounts by eighteen women of how they reached decisions to have, or not to have, children. Stephanie Dowrick and Sybil Grunberg, who edited the book, express the wish that the different accounts will 'convey the complexity' and 'the deep personal significance of the decision whether or not to have children, the most irrevocable and important one that most of us will have to make' (p.8). In the first part of her essay Micheline Wandor tries to recapture and describe the reasons why she became a mother.

● As you read the extract, bear in mind the following questions:

1 Micheline Wandor mentions 'rationales' at several points in the extract. What does she mean by the word? And how have these rationales affected her life?

2 What effects did feminism have on the ways Micheline saw her life?

Extract 6

I am, of course, talking PF – post-feminism. My rationale BF – before feminism – was breathtakingly simple and, as I look back now, it fitted sweetly into the dominant ideology: I was female, liked babies, was frightened at the big wide world, fell in love . . . I *had* wanted to become an actress after university, but I was worried about the prospect of disappearing into obscure repertory. When I tried other jobs and prospective employers suggested I should take a shorthand-typing course – that clinched it. With hindsight and the trauma of a marriage break-up and divorce a certain note of cynicism always creeps into my account of this period in my life; but the fact is that on the whole at that time middle-class women worked despite motherhood not alongside it, and in the face of a cold and hostile world of work, love, marriage, building a home and family were exciting and potentially fulfilling prospects.

In effect I went from one family to another – with only the three years of university in between. I wish I could have avoided that. Compared to many other women (and compared to almost all men) I missed out on those vital few years of coping with an adult life among adults, earning my living as a non-mother. Since I didn't start earning and writing seriously until I was nearly thirty, I reckon I have lost about eight years. It's no good being told that the experiences I have had 'compensate' for those years. Of course at some level my life and work now must be affected by the insights and experiences I had during that time – but it is very hard to work out what the real relationship is. Motherhood is so intense and *private*, so individually experienced, so extraordinary, that I have no real grasp of how it affects the rest of my view of the world – except at occasional moments when symptoms erupt: I get impatient at the 'childish' way a friend is behaving and 'tell her off', or someone sneezes and I offer them a tissue from the store of things I keep in my bag 'just in case'. During the years when my children were small, my handbags seemed to get bigger and bigger. Now that my sons are teenagers (Adam, born 1964, and Ivan, born 1966) my handbags are getting smaller again.

However, despite my 'lost' years, I have never once wished I had not had my children. To wish that would be like wishing they were not alive, and that carries the weight of a kind of blasphemy. I have very often wished I could have suspended their material beings, magically rolled them up and carried them in my head, whole and complex as they concretely are – and then given re-birth to them six or seven years later than I actually did. That way I could have had the best of both worlds – had my work and my children, and we would all have lived happily ever after . . . I forgot: happily ever after is a BF (before feminism) concept.

There were a number of other BF concepts which took me through some of the more difficult times of motherhood – or rather, they were rationales which gently but inevitably bit the dust. First, there was the rationale that having two children was no more work than having one; second, that once both children were at school, life would be miraculously simple; third, that once they no longer needed babysitters, my time would be my own. Two children are, of course, at least twice as much work as one. It is not only the different material and physical demands, but the different emotional needs that literally make motherhood a twenty-four-hour occupation. (They were, of course, often twice as wonderful.) Once the children were at school other challenges appeared: combining work and domestic responsibilities was (and still is) a great strain – even for a relatively privileged working mother such as myself, who can do a large proportion of her work at home. It has been relatively easy for me to cope with ill children, compared with other single mothers who work a nine-to-five equivalent and have no one to call on. The third rationale (what would happen when the children no longer needed babysitters) has also worked out rather differently from how I imagined. It's as though I'm going through a faded second adolescence. I still occasionally feel a thrill of excitement when I stay out until midnight or later, no longer restricted by the costs of babysitters. I find myself looking at my watch as the evening wears on (the curfew conditioning dies hard) and every time I get home I have a sense of relief that the house hasn't burned down. It is amusing to think that as my children live through their adolescence, discovering the adult world properly for the first time, I am rediscovering it for the second time. I have in one sense more time for my work, but I now have the challenge of how to organise a home life with two boys in a way that doesn't make me into a super-heroine – doing all the housework like a 'good Mum' should and producing young males who will always expect women to follow suit. I think, actually, there's no fear that they will remember me as

15

anything like a super-heroine; I am ratty enough about trying to share housework to have scotched that particular myth. My current rationale is that when both sons have left home we will be mature, familiar friends. Perhaps this one is going to be the exception that proves the rule.

The rationales came into being as a kind of compensation for the fact that motherhood wasn't what I had expected – unadulterated wonder. The shock of the isolation and much of the sheer slog and boredom were exacerbated by the fact that I felt I wasn't supposed to feel dissatisfied. One of the liberating discoveries feminism brought me in 1969/70 was that it was all right to complain, to be bitter, frustrated, angry; subterranean discontents, previously only spoken about collusively, half-jokingly to other mothers, suddenly erupted. The discovery that one could develop a critique of the family, the proud defence by many women of their independence, were sources of immense support to me; but ironically, these two elements of feminism also collided. I remember having fierce and supportive discussions with other feminist mothers about how society (that is, other people) should care for and about children. I certainly had a tremendous sense of excitement at the prospect that the transformation of 'the family' was just around the corner. Of course it wasn't; a woman's choice not to be a mother is as intense as a woman's choice to have a child. I had arguments with childless feminists who didn't see why they should 'give up' their time to babysit for others. I wrote a poem out of frustration and anger, which was published in *Spare Rib*, Britain's monthly women's liberation magazine. It earned me some gleeful sympathy from mothers and terse hostility from non-mothers.

I had come slap up against one of the basic contradictions which all socialists face, and women face in particular ways: that which exists between individuals who are able to seize the moment for their liberation, and individuals who are not; between collective action and individual choice, between social and individual transformation. It is the area in which questions of a socialist/feminist ethic appear, to which there are no easy answers. The structure of a woman's life as a mother radically affects the degree to which she can participate in political activity. The fact that feminist as well as left-wing politics tend to be dominated by non-mothers is a reflection of the very real material and emotional gap that exists.

My own attitude is now equally selfish. Whereas when my children were small I was happy to look after other people's kids in return for similar services, now that my children are almost grown-up, I guard my childless moments jealously. I am far from the ideal feminist I searched for years ago: unless it is for a very close friend and a special occasion, there's no way I am going to fit babysitting for others into my life . . . that may change, of course.

After my outburst of resentment at not being immediately liberated from the more oppressive aspects of domestica, I went through a phase of rediscovery of the pleasures of being with my children. I've never been the kind of mother (guilt, guilt) who took her children on exciting and educative trips, or who spent hours playing games and reading to them. But I have a great sense of pleasure in the quite ordinary, domestic minutiae of the harmonious moments of living with other people – and children. The very private, intimate moments (when you're not dog-tired) of feeding a tiny baby in the middle of a very still night are unrepeatable. Similarly, when my children were still at primary school many evenings were cosy, intimate and special times; early supper, eaten together in front of the television, then sitting on the couch, a child on either side of me, my arms round them – the warmth of the closeness to other human beings is a very special aspect of parenthood, also unrepeatable. (pp.134-7)

The 'rationales' Micheline writes about in Extract 6 were her way of resolving difficult choices. In the first paragraph she writes about rationalising her entry into motherhood — 'in the face of a cold and hostile world of work, love, marriage, building a home and family were exciting and potentially fulfilling prospects'. Later she writes about other rationales which took her through some of the more difficult times of motherhood — these emerged as a kind of compensation for the fact that motherhood wasn't unadulterated wonder, as she had expected it to be. Micheline learned to question these rationales, and to express dissatisfaction with motherhood: 'subterranean discontents, previously only spoken about collusively, half-jokingly to other mothers, suddenly erupted'. She discovered a critque of the family and the defence by many women of their independence. These, however, presented Micheline with new problems — because it was very difficult to engage in politics in the public sphere while being constrained within the private world of responsibilities for children.

In Extract 7 from *Why Children?* Micheline Wandor describes her life 'post feminism'. She is now divorced and a single parent to two teenage boys.

Extract 7

The present: 1
The petrol pump in my car packs up. I take the tube home. The Automobile Association is permanently engaged, my local garage too busy to look at the car. It is now mid-afternoon. The garage suggests ways in which I can try and start the car and in the course of the next three hours I make three trips back to try. Futile. Meanwhile the kids are home, flopped after school. Failure and the world flood over me. I collapse into tears. I am useless, there is no supper and how will I ever catch up on all the years I've missed. The television is on and I'm sobbing.
Ivan: Why are you crying?
Me (sob): Because I'm tired and horrible and useless.
Adam: Don't be silly. You're fine, you've got a busy life and you're earning a good living.

Me: But the car's broken down, I'm tired and I haven't got you any supper, and I've got to go out tonight. (*Self-pity sets in.*)
Ivan: We'll have take-away for supper.
Adam: Take a taxi if you're going to be late.
Me (more tears): But what about the vitamins and the proteins and the carbohydrates?
Ivan: We *like* take-away, and anyway I'm going to see Spurs play their last match of the season because I'm a loyal fan, so we'll all be busy.
Me: I'm a terrible mother.
Adam: Bullshit. (*Turns the television up louder.*)
I sniff and dry my eyes, consoled. I look up. There is Ivan, his face red, tears pouring down his cheeks; Adam is sitting on the couch holding a cushion up to his face.

16

Me (surprised): What's wrong?

Ivan: If I see you cry it makes me cry.

Adam (muffled): I'm not crying, I haven't cried for years.

I hug Ivan, kiss away the salt on his warm face, laugh at Adam and we all sit there crying and laughing and nobody would believe how corny and amazing the whole scene is. I love them. We are all extraordinary.

The present: 2

It is Saturday morning. I am exhausted, having spent two weeks in rehearsal of a play of mine. Being a writer is a double-edged thing, producing curious and occasional reverberations with motherhood. Both involve long periods of isolation and tedium; both involve periods spent very intensely with other people, which can be emotionally exhausting.

Quick breakfast, I wince at the mess in the house, and go off to the supermarket for the week's food. Stagger home, to find Ivan watching television. 'At ten o'clock in the bloody morning?' I switch if off; resentful howls, his bedroom door slams shut. I go off for my weekly visit to my parents, telling both kids that I want their rooms cleaned, the living room tidied and the washing-up done by the time I get home. We have a rota for basic housework jobs, with Mum doing the lioness's share, so I reckon that today they can do a bit more than usual. Feminist principles on paper are one thing; application in real life quite another. Do them good.

I arrive home at one-thirty, having bought Cornish pasties for lunch. The living-room now has cereal plates and milk-stained glasses placed at tasteful random. Ivan is lying on the floor, watching a sports programme, Adam is lying on the couch complaining of a backache from his paper round. The kitchen sink is full of plates, empty milk bottles, the waste bin is over-flowing. I sweep into the living-room, switch the bloody television off *again*, appeal to their reason, my full and busy life, their laziness, flipping choice four-letter words into the tirade.

Ivan: But it's not natural for a kid to want to do housework.

Me (screams): It's not natural for people *not* to want to do

housework. *(warning)* You'll be male chauvinists when you grow up.

Ivan (sweet reason): But everyone is male chauvinist.

Me: That's the trouble with everybody; the whole world is unnatural.

Adam has gone silent and by now is in the kitchen, wearing rubber gloves, washing up a glass. He puts it on the draining board. I feel the water. It is cold. I put the glass back in to the sink. He washes it again and puts it back on the draining board. The water is still cold. We repeat the tense silent dance once more, by which time the water is getting lukewarm. I leave him to it.

When he has finished washing up I return to the attack.

Me: You both want me to be your bloody servant.

Adam: Don't worry. I'll leave home soon and then I won't have to think about anyone but me.

Me: Oh yes? Well, you'll find that life isn't bloody like that.

He pulls off the rubber gloves and flings them into the sink so that the insides get wet.

Me: And you haven't taken the empty milk bottles out.

He takes his jacket.

Adam: I'm going out. You may see me tomorrow.

Front door slams. Bloody kids. Bloody hell.

The present: coda

I am working at home. I stop when the kids get back from school and go off to do the shopping. When I get back, the children's eyes light up. They pounce on the bags and packets, dumping them on every available kitchen surface, inspecting goodies for instant gratification and turning over the prospect of the next few days' meals. I am a wonderful mother.

That evening Adam announces he's going out. I suggest he shouldn't be back late. He says he'll do what he wants and reminds me that he doesn't need me to tell him when he's tired, cold, wet or hungry any more. Next morning, as I yawn over breakfast, he tells me I shouldn't have so many late nights. *Touché*. (pp.138–40)

The extract is written almost in the style of play with dramatic scenes framing a kind of monologue. We seem to be reading not a carefully recollected description of past life, but more or less direct transcriptions of present experience. Certainly, as far as we can tell, the experience is closer to the time of writing than in any of the other extracts. You might also catch some echoes of the issues raised at the end of the Virginia Woolf extracts above. Both Micheline Wandor and Virginia Woolf counterpose their accounts of experience with the implicit suggestion that autobiography more usually concentrates on presenting life as an ordered flow of events.

● Before reading on make a note of the similarities and differences that have occurred to you as you have read through the extracts between Micheline Wandor's experiences and those of Mrs Wrigley, Virginia Woolf and May Hobbes. You might find it helpful to look back at your notes comparing Mrs Wrigley and Virginia Woolf and Mrs Wrigley and May Hobbes.

2.5 Dr K. Tandon

Our final extract, Extract 8, is from an article by an Asian doctor, Dr K. Tandon. It was first published in *Spare Rib* in the October 1983 issue which was devoted to black women's issues. We have included this extract in order to take account in some way of the experiences of the substantial number of Asian and Afro-Caribbean women in Britain, and particularly to raise the issue of how far the experiences of these women are affected by racism as well as sexism. Dr Tandon writes particularly of her experience of training and working as a doctor. We would emphasize here that, as with the other extracts in this Section, you are reading of the experiences of a particular woman in a particular situation. Dr Tandon's experiences are no more to be seen as 'typical' of black women's than Virginia Woolf's are typical of white women of her time.

Asian women have come to Britain as workers or more frequently as wives or daughters of immigrant workers. Patterns of migration are complex and change over time. Asian women came from India, Pakistan and Bangladesh in the 1960s and 1970s. They came often from rural peasant societies and in Britain worked in factories. But, in the wake of decolonization, Asian women came also from East Africa where they had been part of business and trading communities. Many people writing about Asian women have emphasized the cultural differences between Asian societies and British society, stressing for example differences in family culture, religion and language, and have isolated Asian women's experiences of arranged marriages, etc. For others it is their position as low-paid workers which is the key issue. There are also substantial numbers of Asian women who were themselves born in Britain.

● As you read through the extract, bear in mind the following questions:

1 Do the experiences described in this extract seem comparable to those described in any of the earlier extracts in this section?

2 Does Dr Tandon speak of racial discrimination in terms of a particular incident or something more general?

Extract 8

From my earliest memory I wanted to be a Doctor. I wanted to make sick people better. I never had any other reason I was aware of that made me go wholeheartedly into spending many years of my life attempting to achieve the professional training that would enable me to give my best. . . . Alas, my naive, starry eyed and idealistic motives did not account for the establishment that makes up the very heart of the British Medical Profession. . . .

Being a non-white female doctor, I have been all too often subjected to discrimination regarding first my colour and then my sex. Most white female doctors I have met are racist, and most of the white male doctors I have met are primarily racist and also sexist. The obstruction to one's training due to the attitudes is veiled in such hypocrisy, my initial reaction was one of total bewilderment; I questioned my own ability, thought I was imagining the discrimination, but over the years a systematic pattern emerged. I thought patients are the whole reason for our existence as a profession and results are there for all to see. I was soon to realise that... the whole profession is based on exclusivity and power. The climb upwards is provided with one hurdle after another, the first being acceptance into medical school. First choices go to white males often from a medical family or from an upper middle class background. I was surprised, but thrilled when I was accepted into medical school. I was told later by a professor that it was unusual to accept a non-white woman but that being articulate in the English language, not having much of a foreign accent and being from a medical family had helped. Discussions with my colleagues revealed that my required grades for entry had been much higher than many of them had been asked for; non-white friends of mine had been rejected with equivalent grades to some of the white males that had been accepted on the course with explanation that their qualifications had not come up to the required standard.

I was one of six women, and four non-white students (the other three were male) in a class of eighty. The course was long, loaded with examinations every few weeks and totally fascinating. I was astounded at the knowledge and skills there were to acquire. I learnt to study tongues and throats, feel livers and bowels, deliver babies, remove lumps and bumps, take and give blood and a multitude of other skills. Encouragement was bountiful and all but two individuals qualified at the end of five and a half years.

It was in the postgraduate period that I found a different situation. After the period in internship when one is a 'House Officer' and may work up to one hundred and forty hours a week doing every day, one night in two and one weekend in two 'on call', there comes a time when the decision as to what field of the vast area one will specialise in must be made. I chose general surgery and got a job at a junior level in a teaching hospital. After completion of one year I was told by my superiors that although I was very competent, general surgery was really a man's speciality and that I would be best advised to go into a peripheral branch of surgery since I would never progress beyond a certain level. The line of argument was that the number of fully qualified women general-surgeons in the United Kingdom can be counted on the fingers of one hand – why not attempt Obstetrics which deals with women or eye surgery which is a little like doing embroidery?

Contracts of jobs in the National Health Service at a junior level extend for a period of six months or one year; more recently two year rotating schemes have been introduced, but these are few in number and are heavily subscribed to, the number of applicants being ten or 20 times the number of jobs available. These two year schemes are often between a group of hospitals to attempt a varied training programme and may involve a lot of travelling in a week.

Since most jobs however are on short term contracts, the possibility for setting up a stable home or having a family with a reasonably settled background is remote. Single women find it difficult to progress in certain chosen specialities, but married women doctors have a real battle on their hands – often being offered part-time jobs on a sessional basis to do outpatient clinics, family planning clinics or general practice sessions. These are often on a locum or temporary basis with poor job security, lack of holiday or sick pay and booked on a week to week basis; cul-de-sac jobs with the prospect of promotion and teaching being nil. The rapport with full-time 'resident' hospital staff is often minimal, the appointment being impersonal. There is a feeling of hopelessness and resentment at being treated as a pair of hands to 'clear' the outpatient clinics with no incentive to keep up with new advances in the subject and the standard of patient care is variable. I did one of these part-time appointments for three months on one occasion and only spoke to the consultant in charge once, the only time he made an appearance in the clinic in that period! The bulk of the work was handled by other part-time staff and any 'interesting' patients were whisked away by the resident doctors; and unless one maintained a very positive and active follow-up system one rarely got any feedback. I have spoken to numerous doctors in a similar position. The senior hospital posts are held by white males by and large and the odd white female; the part-time and temporary posts are held mainly by non-white males and females and married women doctors.

Being of a single-minded nature, I decided to cling onto a surgical speciality and continue with the required postgraduate examinations set by the Royal College of Surgeons. There are equivalent ones in other specialities. The exams are set in two parts, the first being in the basic sciences of the appropriate speciality. If one passes part one, after doing a further two years of the speciality in a recognised post, one is eligible to take the final part. One is charged a handsome fee for the privilege of sitting these examinations; it is forfeited in failure. Senior jobs stipulate the requirement of these postgraduate diplomas, so they are the filters for the individuals who are not considered desirable for promotion. The written papers are branded with anonymity where one is recognised by a number; the clinical and practical parts involve face to face meetings with senior consultants in the speciality who most certainly exercise discrimination of a racist and sexist nature. The candidates who pass average 5 to 10% of the total. On the three occasions I attempted the examination, roughly 80 to 90% of the candidates were non-white. Of the candidates who passed 90% were white and the odd one or two would be a non-white male or a non-white female. These proportions are easily discernible in the working population of the National Health Service, and seem to have remained fairly consistent since I qualified about 10 years ago. Prior to that it was worse. I now have the full postgraduate requirements to be eligible for surgical jobs at a senior level. I am still looking for one although white female doctors I taught as medical students have often been appointed to posts for which I have been turned down. I have checked my references which have been excellent; I can only come to one conclusion that I am discriminated against on the grounds of being non-white, or a woman, or both. Temporary appointments are fairly easy to come by, covering for another doctor on holiday or maternity leave, etc. One is handling patients, performing operations and procedures as if one were doing a permanent job, but this remains elusive.

You might have compared Dr Tandon's account with that of either Micheline Wandor or May Hobbes. You might perhaps have thought that Dr Tandon's job as a surgeon makes her more likely to be identified with the educated middle class, a social group which also includes writers. But Dr Tandon's job seems to involve so much temporary or part-time work that a comparison with May Hobbes may seem more appropriate. Certainly race and racial discrimination are key features of Dr Tandon's article. She claims particular discrimination in connection with individual job applications and also a general discrimination within the medical profession and in society. You will see from Section 6 of this Unit that people have considered sex discrimination in similar terms. Dr Tandon's account is designed to highlight racism and sexism; she chooses the experiences she wishes to describe accordingly, omitting most of her 'private life'. As a piece of polemic, comparison with the extract by Mrs Wrigley might seem appropriate, although the tone of the extract is very different.

2.6 Consideration of the extracts

If you look back at p.6 you will recall that we asked you to think about some questions as you read through the extracts. We asked you to consider what aspects of the woman's life seem most important in the extract, what similarities and differences between the women's lives struck you as you read through the extracts, and what might explain any differences between the women's lives which occurred to you. We have deliberately refrained from giving you our own views about the differences and similarities between the different women's lives, because there are no 'correct' answers. You may well find that you have picked out different features from those found by some of your fellow students, perhaps as a result of your own particular background and experiences.

You might, for instance, have commented on the differences between the women, noting, for example, the different kinds of educational opportunities open to them; or the relative freedom which Virginia Woolf had to pursue her education and writing; or the flexibility which being a writer gave Micheline Wandor in organizing her life, in contrast with the long hours of manual work which Mrs Wrigley and May Hobbes had to do to make ends meet. Another difference you might have picked out was the different attitudes which the women express towards marriage. Mrs Wrigley writes about marriage as if it were quite harmonious, whereas Micheline Wandor and May Hobbes write about the contradiction between their expectations of marriage and how they experienced it. Or you might have thought that Dr Tandon's experiences were different because she experienced racism as well as sexism; her experiences may seem more akin to those of May Hobbes than those of a white woman doctor.

You might, on the other hand, have noticed some similarities running through the extracts. You might have noted a number of references to the limited employment opportunities available to women, especially if employment has to be combined with looking after children. But the extracts by Mrs Wrigley and May Hobbes also testify to the importance of women's earnings in supporting the family. In the case of Mrs Wrigley and May Hobbes, work outside the home led to radical activity.

Another similarity you might have noticed is that all the women write about women's lives in a way that implies criticism of the role ascribed to women and rejection of the stereotyped attitudes held about women. All the women stress the importance of changing the position of women in work, the family and society in general, but again you probably noticed that each has different ideas about what they think needs changing in response to the different problems they perceive. Dr Tandon is particularly critical of the institution that controls her working life, and the white male-dominated medical establishment. Mrs Wrigley stresses the difficulties arising from poverty, whereas Virginia Woolf stresses the power of the Victorian middle-class family to stifle women.

2.7 Constructing an autobiography

We suggested at the beginning of this Section that the different women writing have constructed an account of their lives, selecting consciously or unconsciously which details to include and how to represent these. The extracts from Virginia Woolf and Micheline Wandor, in particular, draw the reader's attention to the processes of selection and construction which have entered into their own accounts of themselves. It is important to recognize that even an autobiography, which on the face of it seems to be a simple expression of a person's identity, involves selection from experience and construction of an identity. It is important to read accounts of women's experience with an awareness of this, perhaps to see an autobiographical account more as a 'representation' of experience rather than as an account of the 'real self'. Elizabeth Wilson reflects on similar questions towards the end of her autobiography, *Mirror Writing*:

> There is no simple reflection of oppression. We think of writing as putting a mirror to the world, and imagine that our readers will see in the mirror what we see. But the mirror is more like a prism. The image changes shape and flashes off in all directions in its collision with the reader's consciousness. The reader always sees something of herself in our mirror . . .
>
> Personal identity may be no more than a mirage, simply the longing to crack the mirror in order to find out what lies behind it. Ultimately the quality, flavour and nature of 'my identity' must remain a mystery, either because it is too various or because it is simply not there.
>
> Yet even if identity is like one of those sets of Russian dolls, where to open one is to find another inside with at the heart of the smallest — emptiness, we continue to search. Even if 'my identity' is a discourse of fragments and self-contradiction, I have a subjective sense of coherence and continuity, equally though of distance and of difference (was that really me?). That is the strangeness of identity, that we experience ourself as both fragmentary *and* coherent. (pp.156–7)

2.8 Summary

Our aim in this Section has been to consider how women write about their experience as women. We have suggested, in the concluding pages, that the process by which people write about their experiences inevitably involves selection and construction, and that an autobiographical account can perhaps be best understood as a representation of experience rather than a straightforward transpostion of experience into words. Despite this, we think that a good deal about women's experience and how it has changed can be learned from reading autobiographical accounts.

In Section 3 we approach the question of women's experience again, but this time from rather a different angle. We consider how women are written about in the press.

Women in newspapers

In this Section we consider how women's experiences are represented in a selection of daily national newspapers. In order to work through this Section you will need a copy of a daily newspaper. You can either use an issue of your regular paper, or else one that is unfamiliar to you. Our aim is to look in some detail at how women are written about in newspapers, and we shall be concerned with the following questions: What kinds of women are written about? On what pages do articles about women appear? Are women written about differently in different newspapers? Are women represented in stereotypical ways, or in ways that are different from those in which men are represented?

● We shall start our analysis of women in newspapers by asking you to undertake an exercise for yourself. Work through the newspaper you have chosen and answer the following questions:

1 How many separate items are there in your paper:
(a) predominantly or exclusively about women?
(b) predominantly or exclusively about men?
(c) equally about men and women?
(d) about no human character at all?

2 How many named individuals of each sex are referred to in your paper? Divide your results according to the various sections of the paper, i.e. news and gossip pages, women's pages, letters, sport, business pages.

3 Who are the 'women in the news'? Work through the paper, section by section, listing the women who feature in the news and what they do that is considered news-worthy.

4 How often are women-attached-to-men written about? Note down the women who appear in the paper *only* because they are attached to men (without whom they probably would not have attracted the publicity).

5 How often are the women mentioned in stories, features, etc. associated with paid employment? Make a note of the occupations mentioned.

TABLE 1

		I		II		III
		Daily Mail (23.3.82)		Guardian (28.1.81) and Sunday Times (25.1.81)		
1	Items: about women	18		4		
	about men	59		43		
	about men and women	17		12		
	about no human	15		3		
		109		62		
2	Named individuals mentioned	Men	Women	Men	Women	
	news/gossip pages	98	18			
	women's pages	2	3			
	letters	3	6	No breakdown		
	sport	78	—			
	business	12	—			
		193	27	385	33	
3	Women in the news	Princess of Wales Mrs Thatcher Mrs Ghandi First TAVR Colonel Greenham Common CND		'Political, i.e. Mrs Thatcher Mrs Williams' No further detail but politics accounted for 12 out of 33 women named.		
4	Women-attached-to men	Princess of Wales Lady Howe Danuta Walesa Wife of winning gambler Wife of buyer of house next to Prince and Princess of Wales estate		6 out of 33 women named		
5	Women's employment	Prime Minister (2) Bass guitarist Dinner ladies School teacher Pilot Actress TV producer		3 actresses 2 other unspecified		

We did the same exercise ourselves, using the *Daily Mail* for Tuesday 23 March, 1982. The exercise is based on a similar one reported by Anne Coote and Beatrix Campbell in their book about women's liberation called *Sweet Freedom*. They looked at two national newspapers in January, 1981, the *Guardian* of 28 January and the *Sunday Times* of 25 January. In Table 1 we list the results of our analysis of the *Daily Mail* in Column 1, and the results of Coote and Cambell's spot check in Column 2. We have left the third column blank for you to write in your findings.

Certain conclusions spring to mind from our analysis of the *Daily Mail* for 23 March 1982. First, women are written about considerably less than men. However, certain women are given prominence: Mrs Thatcher, for instance, and the Princess of Wales, who receives almost saturation coverage. Other, less prominent, women are given considerable coverage in the *Mail's* Female section, which contains one full-page article about 'probably the only woman who has competed successfully in the male-dominated champagne-and-cigar world of executive air travel'. Women hardly figure in the mass of smaller news items, which many people would consider to be the bulk of the paper, and they are completely absent from the sports and city pages. A number of times, women featuring in the news are attached to (and generally married to) news-worthy men. Lady Howe, for instance – who used to be the Deputy Chairman of the Equal Opportunities Commission but gave up this when her husband became Chancellor of the Exchequer — appears in the news because she is going to enrol at the London School of Economics to do a degree. However, the news story only mentions Lady Howe's own career in the final paragraph (Extract 9).

Frequently, when woman are mentioned in the news, in the *Mail* they are given different treatment from men. Four women employees who appealed to an industrial tribunal because they were sacked for refusing to join a closed shop are referred to in the heading of the story as 'Dinner Ladies' and their story is placed on a page

Extract 9

She'll show him Howe!

The Howes: She will be economically independent

OUR embattled Chancellor of the Exchequer Sir Geoffrey Howe, 55, will soon be able to get economic advice from his wife Elspeth—at 50 she is enrolling at the prestigious London School of Economics in October.

Lady Howe hopes to do a three-year degree course in Social Administration.

Although she lacks the present-day qualifications of 'O' and 'A' levels — she left Wycombe Abbey public school with Ordinary School Certificate (the forerunner of 'O' levels)—it is virtually certain she will be accepted.

'She is very powerful in her own right,' said the University Pro-Director Professor Alan Day. 'I think we are lucky to have her.'

Her application has still to be scrutinised by the committee which decides whether a mature student's qualifications and experience are comparable to today's 'A' level passes. But the word is that she will get through.

'In a way I am starting back to front,' said Lady Howe, a mother of three who married Sir Geoffrey in 1953.

'I am quite sure that young people with their ideas and their ideals will be fascinating, though I expect there will be some differences of view between us.'

One of the reasons Lady H is undertaking what would be a gruelling academic chore for a young person, is that she finds life as the Chancellor's wife rather restricting.

She had to give up being deputy Chairman of the Equal Opportunities Commission; and although she is a magistrate and serves on many committees, this course—which includes economics—will challenge her mind.

23

containing two other stories about women (and a third story about Dame Edna Everage). And Jean Blackwood, the first woman to command a full regiment in the Territorial Army, is described taking her command for the first time. The article then says that 'she went home to cook the dinner' and devotes a whole paragraph to her domestic arrangements (Extract 10).

Extract 10

Jean signals start of a new Army order

JEAN BLACKWOOD yesterday became the first woman to command a full regiment in the Army. Then she went home to cook the dinner.

Lieutenant Colonel Blackwood, 37, took command of more than 500 men, eight officers and 100 women volunteers of the Territorial Army 37th (Wessex and Welsh) Signal Regiment based at Bristol.

The new CO, married to a music lecturer, said: 'I like the challenge of my Army job and it doesn't really clash with my domestic situation. My husband can cook but I prefer to do it because I'm a better cook than he is. But we both do the dishes.'

She has been a Territorial since 1962 and the unit's second in command for two years. 'I don't think of myself as being a woman when I am doing the job,' she said. 'I think of the job.'

As you may have noticed if you read through the cutting yourself, Jean Blackwood comments that she doesn't think of herself as being a woman when she is doing the job, as if 'being a woman' and 'doing a job' are incompatible with one another.

This kind of treatment, which makes reference to women's personal and domestic circumstances, is not reserved exclusively for women in this edition of the *Mail*. A man who bought a cottage so as to be a near neighbour of the Prince and Princess of Wales was described as having 'a flock of grey hair surmounting the amused face of an incurable eccentric'. But such a case is rare. Generally it is stories about women which are embellished with personal and domestic details.

To what extent does the treatment of women vary from one newspaper to another? If you read the *Daily Telegraph* or the *Sun* you may find that your results are rather different from ours. You may also find that your results differ if you look at the *Daily Mail* in subsequent years. On 23 March 1982 there is considerable overlap in the main items about women covered and the ways they are covered in the 'popular' press *(Sun, Star, Mirror, Mail* and *Express),* although only the *Sun* and the *Star* contain full-length pictures of a naked woman to titillate their readers. Generally, the 'serious' press *(Times, Telegraph, Guardian)* have fewer items about women than the popular papers, a fact which Anna Coote and Beatrix Campbell comment on in their spot checks of the papers. Of these 'serious' papers, only the *Guardian* has a woman's page, which, on 23 March 1982 is devoted entirely to consumer affairs.

24

The 'serious' press, when it does report items concerning women, pays little or no attention to their domestic or sex lives, in contrast to the popular press. The coverage of Jean Blackwood differs in this respect between 'popular' and 'serious' papers. The *Express*, *Mail* and *Mirror* all make reference to the fact that she goes home and washes the dishes. *The Times* makes a passing reference to her husband and to the fact that she has no children, while the *Guardian* says nothing about her domestic circumstances.

In covering the case of the women canteen workers, only *The Times* carries an account written as a straightforward industrial relations story. *The Times* is the only paper which refers to the women as 'women' in its heading; the other papers call them 'dinner ladies' and several make a play on the domestic nature of their work.

3.1 A feminist analysis of the press

Feminist have often been very critical of the press, arguing that newspapers produce distorted and stereotyped representations of women. Extract 11 gives the conclusions Anna Coote and Beatrix Campbell draw from their study:

Extract 11

The pattern remains typical of news coverage throughout the media – especially in the 'serious' newspapers, and on radio and television. A 1980 study of one local station, Radio Nottingham, has found that men's voices occupy seven-eighths of the two-and-a-half-hour morning news programme. Women are featured more regularly in the 'popular' press, but these are almost invariably 'wives', 'mums', 'brides', 'mistresses', victims of crime or misfortune, TV stars, or 'sizzlers'. Reports are written from a male perspective, almost obliterating female experience. When a woman, a man and two children died together in a caravan fire in January 1981, the *Daily Mirror* told its readers: 'An RAF officer and his family were found dead...' Women as autonomous human beings rarely feature anywhere in the news media. Their multi-faceted experience as women (individually and collectively) is seldom reported at all – and almost never from a female perspective.

A standard response to criticism of this kind is that women don't get mentioned as often as men because they don't do as many important things. That is true enough – if one accepts the Fleet Street definition of what is important. Where does that definition come from? Who has decided what is 'news' and what is not; what is a 'hard' story and what is a 'soft' one; what is central and what is peripheral? Who has set the standards by which certain everyday events, but not others, have become 'human interest stories', worthy of public attention?

The prevailing values of the news media have not fallen from heaven into the laps of editors: they have been manufactured over the years by successive generations of middle-class newspapermen, who have handed them down, intact, to their counterparts in radio and television. So solidly have these values been established that it has become hard to imagine any other way of conveying information. Most journalists sincerely believe that there is such a thing as 'objective' or 'unbiased' reporting, when in fact the most they can do is to communicate events as fairly as possible, from their own point of view, according to the journalistic conventions they have learned,

and in a manner which is acceptable to their editors. For their readers, listeners and viewers, the product of journalism *becomes the real world* – even though it is nothing more than one cockeyed version of it.

More women have gradually become involved in journalism but they have never been able to set the pace, or imprint their character on the news industry. They have always lacked the power to challenge the dominant view of what matters, or develop a tradition of reporting which consistently interprets events through their eyes.

To make it in journalism, women have to strive to be as good as men, according to male standards. This is not easy, and so women have remained, throughout the 1970s, in a minority in journalism, occupying the lowest-paid and least influential jobs. A 1977 survey by the National Union of Journalists found that among 314 journalists employed on seven newspapers in the North of England, 279 were men and 35 were women. All editors and deputies were male; all sports specialists were male; all photographers but one were male; there were 69 male and 11 female sub-editors; 42 male and eight female features/specialist writers; and 99 male and 23 female reporters. That pattern has changed very little – nor is it substantially different in other parts of the country, or in radio or television. Our spot check on the *Guardian* and *Sunday Times* in 1981 found a total of 11 female and 74 male by-lines.

With the arrival of women's movement has come a growing awareness that certain items are being left off the news agenda. The media have made minor adjustments but have managed all the while to identify women as a sub-category of a male universe – both in the style of reporting and in the allocation of space. Thus, a news report will inform us that 'many people, including women' have been injured in an accident. News editors feel free to insist that one story about women is quite enough for one day. Television executives may arrange for an occasional documentary on women, or even an occasional series. But they retain a clear view that programmes about women have their special place and can be over-done.

● In the light of your own newspaper analysis and the evidence from our analysis of the *Daily Mail* for 23 March 1982, do you find Coote and Campbell's arguments convincing? Consider particular their arguments on two points.

(a) Do you agree with their assertions about what is defined as newsworthy and with their analysis of the values underlying newsworthiness in the first three paragraphs? Or do you think on the basis of the evidence you have collected that they overstate their case?

(b) If you look at the remaining paragraphs of the extract you will see that Coote and Campbell argue that it is because men control the media and men write most of the news stories that women are marginalized. Now look back at the newspaper that you have analysed and count how many items in it are written by men, how many are written by women and how many are uncredited.

Our findings from the *Daily Mail* for 23 March 1982 are given in Column 1 of Table 2. In Column II we have written in Coote and Campbell's findings. We have again left Column III blank for you to write in your own findings.

TABLE 2

	I *Daily Mail* (23.3.82)	II *Guardian* (28.1.81) *Sunday Times* (25.1.81)	III
Items written by men	43	74	
Items written by women	5	11	
Uncredited	53	Figure not quoted	

● Do you think Coote and Campbell are right to argue that it is because men are in positions of power in the mass media that women are represented in particular ways in newspapers?

The question of why women are represented in the newspapers in particular ways, and in ways that are different from the ways in which men are represented, is a very important question. Coote and Campbell provide one kind of explanation as to why women are represented differently. You might have thought of other, alternative, explanations. You might think that the newspapers are simply *reflecting and reproducing* the prevailing values of our society. Or that women are represented in particular ways in order to increase newspaper sales. We shall come back to this question of alternative explanations in Section 6.

For the moment we want to emphasize three points. First, that the question which Coote and Campbell raise, and which we have asked you to think about here, is an example of a very important question which will recur in different forms throughout the Course. Second, Coote and Campbell provide one kind of explanation as to *why* women are represented differently within newspapers. There are, however, *alternative explanations*. This suggests that there is no single 'correct' explanation of why women are represented differently, but rather an array of possible explanations. Third, different explanations have different implications for social change. If, for instance, you think that it is because *men* control and predominate in newspaper offices that women are represented in particular ways, this would suggest that getting more women into journalism, and particularly into positions of power within newspapers, would result in changes in the ways in which women are represented. If, on the other hand, you think that newspapers simply reflect and reproduce the prevailing values of society, then it seems to be relatively unimportant whether it is men or women who control the newspapers and write news stories. In this case, it is the prevailing values of society that needs to be changed, rather than the people who work in the newspaper

—SORRY, BUT WE ALREADY HAVE ONE LADY REPORTER

industry. Finally, if you think it is because of the economic structure of society that the newspaper industry represents women in a particular way, then it would seem to follow that it is necessary to change the economic structure in order to change the ways in which newspapers represent women. We shall come back to these questions in Section 6, where we examine some of the alternative explanations in more detail. In Section 4 we consider women's experience from another angle, looking, this time, at how women are represented in advertisements.

Advertisements construct women

In exploring how women are written about in newspapers in Section 3, we have concentrated (apart from a passing reference to female nudes in the *Sun* and the *Star*) on how women's experiences are *written about*. In this Section we continue our exploration of how women are represented in the mass media by turning to visual representations, and specifically to advertisements.

● If you have a magazine, or colour supplement, or mail order catalogue to hand, we would like you to look at it and see what kind of images of women prevail in the advertisements in it. You could do this by counting how many times you find advertisements showing women cooking or preparing food, caring for children, looking after their husbands, doing a job or engaging in leisure activities.

Images of women in advertisements have been the subject of a good deal of controversy and analysis, and a number of people have written about the principal ways in which women are represented in advertisements. The following extracts provide two different analyses of images of women in advertisements. The first, by a journalist, Carolyn Faulder, comes from an article on advertising in a book on images of women in the media called *Is this your Life?* published in 1977:

> In recent years it is woman as housewife who has been the object of unremitting study, discussion and marketing attack. Let's get it straight. It is not her role which is being called into question, but her amazing potential as the major buyer in our society, who spends £80 out of every £100 laid out on consumer goods. Half the savings in building societies are put there by women, and women are half the shareholders in this country. Her family structure, her housekeeping budget, her shopping patterns, her cooking skills, her eating habits, her division of her time, her social attitudes, her reading and leisure interests, her views on branded products, and her 'need' for new products have been carefully researched, analysed and monitored. . . (p.37)
>
> The single female stereotype which, more than any other, infuriates women viewers, and not just those who declare themselves to be feminists, is the domestic skivvy image that dominates so much household advertising. It is all very well for career women in advertising to protest (and they do) that these are domestic products so the kitchen and the home are the natural ambience in which to proclaim their virtues. True enough, but it is the tone of voice and the absurd expectations so often suggested by the advertisement to be the housewife's *raison d'être*, which are so unacceptable . . . Servility oozes out of television advertising, exemplified by all those ads for household products which show mum dancing attendance on her family; if she does get any assistance it invariably comes from her daughter, who is growing up to a 'proper little mother'. (p.45–6)

The second extract comes from a book called *Woman's Estate* by Juliet Mitchell:

> it is not just in London's King's Road that the 'right' anything or nothing goes. It is as hard *not* to keep up with the changing (and multiple) fashions as it is to keep up with them. Beauty is all, in this epoch of loving and expansive narcissism. The commercial 'exploitation' (which comes first?) of this is phenomenal. The ex-Empire (or its remains) has been reraided to reproduce itself in miniature concentration in Oxford Street: you can eat, dress and adorn — Indian, old Chinese, Arabian, African . . . And having been offered all possibilities for self-glorification, having produced the sexually radiant you, the commercial dimension of capitalism can re-use you; this time you, yourself, will do to sell the drabber products: cars, washing machines, life insurance. No city in the world boasts such a density of 'sexual objectification' on its bill-boards and subway ads, as does London. (p.141)

Faulder argues that women are mainly represented in a housewife role, working as a 'domestic skivvy', serving the family. The Brabantia advertisement (Figure 1) is a bald instance of the kind of image of a women that Faulder is writing about.

Mitchell, on the other hand, emphasizes the importance of sexual objectification of women in advertisements. By this she means that women are used as sex objects in order to sell commodities. Representations of women as sexy and glamorous can be used to sell products to women, as in the Badedas advertisement (Figure 2), or to men, as in the Pioneer advertisement (Figure 3).

● Now think about the adequacy of Faulder's and Mitchell's analyses. Do you find either argument convincing? If you managed to look at a magazine of your own, consider the ads in it and think about whether either Faulder's or Mitchell's arguments make sense of these.

One of the criticisms which you might have made of Faulder's and Mitchell's arguments is that they are out of date, or oversimplifying. Surely, you might say, women are represented in a wider variety of ways then Faulder and Mitchell suggest? And even if they were not in the early 1970s, they are now, with many more women earning a wage and many people having a much greater awareness of women's independence?

4.1 Recent changes in advertisements

Jo Spence, a photographer who is interested in representations of women, suggests that there have been some changes in these representations since the mid-1970s. The following extract is taken from a paper by her called, 'What do people do all day?':

> . . . From about 1976 onwards . . . I have noticed some gradual changes. These do not only appear in the more 'positive' imagery in magazines for younger women . . . It is acknowledged that not everything in the female garden is lovely. Family life may be cracking apart at a few of the seams at least. Women have problems because of the lack of child care facilities, they worry about pay, working conditions and price rises, they suffer from increasing isolation and alienation, and sometimes violence. The problems of 'love and sex' continue, of course, but also take on new forms — 'Is my wife really a homosexual?' wrote one demented husband recently. Occasionally women are shown getting together to tackle particular issues, but more often it is *individual* problems and hardships that are highlighted. Interspersed with all this are the lives of royalty, the stars and other 'great people': they are naturalistically represented as 'just like our family', facing the same problems that we all do. In the emerging narrative, then, women can be financially independent (or at least major contributors to the family budget), they can make their own decisions about their leisure time, they can instigate relationships and need not be passive sexually . . .
>
> . . . One development is that, although women continue to *display* themselves, they do so in a wider variety of locations — particularly the previously 'male' world of paid work and active leisure. (pp.32–4)

Jo Spence says that in the Halifax Building Society's campaign which ran through 1977 and 1978, for the first time in contemporary advertising it is an identifiable 'worker' who advises us where to save our money (Figure 4). This contrasts with the Halifax's previous long-running campaign which had hinged explicitly around 'love' and 'security'. Spence writes:

> Thus the secretary at work is a striking change from the crude studio set-ups in which a man's hands were seen placing an engagement ring on a woman's well manicured finger with the legend 'Promise. Confidence. Security'. (p.34)

The advertisement for Boots sanitary products also show the women in a more active mode, this time in the previously 'male' world of active leisure (Figure 5).

Spence suggests, however, that these new ways of representing women are not unambiguous, since the woman is still represented in terms of beauty, glamour and sexuality. She concludes the passage in which she says that 'although women continue to *display* themselves, they do so in a wider variety of locations' in the following ways: 'In many of these it is still beauty, glamour and sexuality that are emphasised —

FIGURE 1

FIGURE 2

FIGURE 3

FIGURE 4

perhaps women are more 'exciting' when not domestically trapped.' 'But', she continues, 'there is also a growing emphasis on self-gratification in place of the former mixture of dedicated service to men and children with a narcissistic attitude to self, (p.34).

FIGURE 5

Judith Williamson, who writes specifically about advertisements, points to another recent trend. She suggests that the women's movement, which has itself been critical of the ways in which women have been represented in advertisements, has also provided material for advertisers:

> To take just one example, the movement of 'Women's Lib' has provided advertisements, one of the most sexist fields of communication there is, with a vast amount of material which actually enhances their sexist stance. There is a television ad for an aftershave 'Censored' where a woman is beating a man at chess. But then he puts on the aftershave and she is so wildly attracted to him that she leaps up, knocking over the chess board where she had him check-mated, and jumps on him like a wild animal. Now, far from the effect being to make us realise how inadequate the man is if he cannot stand being beaten at chess by a woman, her 'cool' and intelligence and obviously 'liberated' image are in fact made to devalue themselves: because the point is that *even* a cool 'dominating' woman, an intellectual threat to a man, even she will become little more than an animal, and a captivated one, on smelling 'Censored' cologne for men. It is obviously more of an achievement to win over a 'liberated' women than one who was submissive all along. Many advertisements are based on this sort of line: 'she's liberated *but . . .*' (pp.170–1).

It seems, then, as if there may be more variety in the ways in which women have been represented in advertisements in recent years. You might like to think about how far these new images still depict circumscribed roles, and how far they represent a real break from the kinds of representation that Faulder and Mitchell identify.

4.2 Ads construct their audience

So far we have written about advertisements as if people are passive viewers who respond to the image that is represented in an advertisement as it passes them by. Advertisements, however, are quite carefully constructed so as to appeal to a specific audience — an audience which is differentiated according to gender, and often according to race and social class. They also help to construct the audience they appeal to by creating particular kinds of desires for specific products or services, thus encouraging people to consume them.

● Turn back for a minute to the advertisements printed in the text so far – Brabantia, Pioneer, Badedas, Halifax, and Boots, who do you think each ad is designed to appeal to? Make a note of what leads you to your particular conclusion in each case.

In some of these advertisements the audience is self-evident. The Brabantia advertisement is directed at the woman as housewife, and the Badedas and Boots advertisements are also clearly addressed to women. The Halifax advertisement too is addressed to women, but this advertisement appeals to the woman who wants her own home and who is concerned about getting good interest on her investment. The appeal here is to the professional woman. The Pioneer advertisement is addressed to a man, however. You can tell from the technical language in which the Pioneer car stereo is described.

Quite often the imagery in advertisements works to construct its audience in much more subtle ways than in the advertisements we have discussed so far. Many advertisements manage to make quite clear to whom they are addressed without giving a full-scale representation of who the person is supposed to be. They invariably manage to convey the gender* of the person they are addressing, by a fleeting suggestion or by representing only a small part of the anatomy.

● Look at the advertisements for Rothman's cigarettes and for Bird's custard (Figures 6 and 7). Each of these contains a hand but no other part of the anatomy. Make a note of which of these advertisements is intended to appeal to women and which to men. Think about what associations the ad makes which lead you to think this.

FIGURE 6   FIGURE 7

*Strictly speaking, the term *gender* refers to the social division between women and men. Whereas *sex* refers to the *biological division between female and male*, the term *gender* refers to the *social or cultural categories of feminity and masculinity*, which are based upon, but are not reducible to, the biological division between female and male. The concepts of sex and gender are discussed in detail by Lynda Birke in Unit 2. You will find the terms *sex* and *gender* recurring throughout the course. Some unit authors differentiate between *sex* and *gender* strictly, whereas others use the terms interchangeably.

Quite clearly the Rothman's ad is designed to appeal to men, whereas the Bird's custard ad is intended for women. The implication in the Rothman's ad is that the man who smokes Rothmans is like a 'world leader', the cigarette and the man add status to each other. In the Bird's ad, by contrast, the woman's hand is synonymous with home. 'Home-made goodness' is conjured up by the plain hand but also by the unadorned plate, the old-fashioned English pudding and by the custard itself.

The fact that advertisements are addressed to a specific audience which is differentiated according to gender but that the ways in which audience is addressed can be quite subtle, is well illustrated in the advertisement for Fiat cars (Figure 8). The advertisement proclaimed 'if it were a lady it would get it's bottom pinched'. It was defaced by the following statement: 'If this lady was a car she'd run you down' — a rejoinder which reversed the advertiser's verbal play. The defacement makes quite clear that the original advertisement was addressed to a man — who else would appreciate the reference to ladies getting their bottoms pinched? The defacement also makes clear that the person reading the advertisement who defaced it was a woman, hence the reference to 'if this lady was a car...'.

FIGURE 8

4.3 Reversal

We have in this Section suggested that women are represented in certain stereotyped ways in advertisements, and that the ways in which notions of gender are appealed to can be quite subtle. The Birds custard ad suggests that you do not have to see a whole picture of a woman as a housewife (as in the Brabantia ad) to make the association of woman with housewife, but that the association can be suggested in more subtle ways. The particular kinds of representation made in ads — of the woman as housewife, or as sex objects are quite specific to women. Although men are also represented in stereotyped ways in ads these are quite different from the ways in which woman are represented. This becomes particularly evident if you try a simple exercise of reversal, that is, if you substitute a man for a woman in an advertisement. In an essay on 'Eroticism and Female Imagery in Nineteenth Centry Art' Linda Nochlin published a nineteenth-century soft porn print entitled 'Achetez de Pommes' (buy some apples) and juxtaposed it with a photograph of a man she had posed carrying instead a tray of bananas (Figure 9).

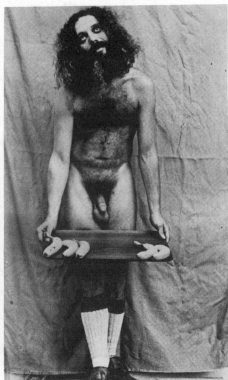

FIGURE 9

Griselda Pollock, who uses this example in an article called 'What's Wrong with Images of Women?' comments on the two photographs in the following terms:

> The usual reaction to this comparison is laughter, an embarrassed reaction to the recognition of that which we take for granted in the 19th century print. This does, of course, invite some comment on its 'sexist' nature but it is nonetheless so naturalised that it is hard to isolate the precise ideological implications of such an image. On an obvious level, as Nochlin points out, while there exists a long tradition of association between female breasts and genitals with fruit which renders the sight of breasts nestling amongst a tray of apples and the implied sale-ability of both unsurprising, no such precedents exist for a similar juxaposition of a penis and its fruity analogue, the banana. However what is more significant in this comparison is precisely the failure of the reversal. It is clear that a bearded man with a silly expression, woolly socks and moccassins does not suggest the same things as the sickly smile of the booted and black stockinged woman not simply because there is no comparable tradition of erotic imagery addressed to women but rather because of the particular signification of women as body and as sexual.

Griselda Pollock also discusses a second set of reversals. In 1973 *Women's Report* published a reversal of the then current Bayer advertisement on the Seven Ages of Man posing a young man in exactly the same position as the ad had placed an adolescent girl and changing the gender of the pronouns in the accompanying copy which then read:

> Adolescence — a time of misgiving. Doubts about the site offered by parents to build a life on. Both head and heart subject to a tyranny of hormones. Youth under stress in search of an identity.
>   B... is there to help *him* through this period of self-seeking. With textile fibres and dyestuffs for the fashionable clothes *he* needs to wear ... With raw ingredients for the cosmetics *he* uses to create *his* own personality. And with simple remedies too. Like aspirin... for the pain *he* will experience.

●The ads are shown in Figure 10. This time we would like you to think about the reversal. Make a few notes on whether or not you think it works, and why.

We think that the reversal doesn't work and that the reason for its failure tells you something important about the differences in the ways in which women and men are

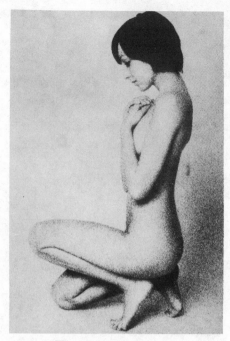

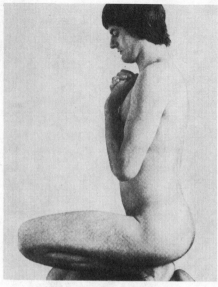

Test-tube baby

Test-tube baby

FIGURE 10

represented in ads. In the original ad there was a strong association suggested between femaleness and nudity. This is broken when the woman is replaced by a man; the man looks silly rather than masculine!

4.4 Summary

We have in this Section considered some of the ways in which women are represented in advertisements, and we have suggested that women tend to be represented as housewives and/or sex objects. Clearly there have been some changes in the representations over the past ten years or so, but women are still depicted in a limited array of roles. You may have noticed some common themes running through this Section and the previous Section on newspapers. We have suggested that women are written about, or depicted, in stereotypical ways and that these are different from the ways in which men are written about and depicted. Great emphasis is placed on the woman's role as sex object, housewife and mother and little emphasis is placed on women's role as wage-earners (the Halifax ad would seem to be the exception rather than the rule). Little attention is paid to women as independent beings — independent, that is, from men or from the family.

People writing about the processes whereby women's experience is represented in partial and stereotyped ways have often used the concept *social construction.* The words *social* and *construction* taken separately should give you some idea about what the concept means. *Construction* suggests that the account of women's experience which you encounter, say, in newspapers or ads, is (a) selected and (b) put together. The accounts you find in these media are not simple *reflections* of women's experience. This is why we have used the term *representation* rather than *reflection* in our discussion. The term *social* suggests that this process of construction takes place within a social context. In contemporary Britain this social context is one in which there are differences in the roles ascribed to women and men (women's primary role being that of housewife and mother, and men's that of wage-earner). There are also inequalities between the sexes.

So far in the Unit we have been concerned with women's experience, with how we can find out about it and how it is represented. We started off by considering how women write about their own experiences. We then looked at how women's experience is represented in newspapers and in advertisements. In the remaining Sections of the Unit our focus shifts. Section 4 is concerned with statistical evidence about the position of women in contemporary British society.

5 Statistical quiz

In this Section we want to look briefly at women's situation in contemporary British society, at differences in the relative positions of women and men, and at inequalities between the sexes. We focus upon four areas — public life, employment and training, education, and the family and the household. You may notice as you work through the Section that these are not really self-contained divisions, and that a number of the questions cross-cut the categories.

DO YOU HAVE A PROPER JOB?

We want you to think about the statistical evidence by doing a quiz. Work through the Sections 5.1 to 5.4, trying to answer all the questions. Start by trying to answer the questions in Section 5.1 on public life. When you have worked through this Section, find the answers on p.37. After checking your answers, move on to the Section 5.2, and so on, until you have worked through the four Sections. Our aim in devising this quiz is to provide a means for you to check your knowledge about the situation of women in contemporary British society. Don't worry if you don't get many answers right. And don't try and learn the statistics by heart. By the time you've worked through the Section, we hope you will have jolted your memory, and perhaps got a slightly better idea of some of the differences between the situations of women and men in contemporary British society.*

5.1 Public life

1 The number of women standing for Parliament has nearly trebled between 1951–79. Has the number of women elected as MPs over that period:

(a) stayed the same   (b) doubled   (c) trebled?

2 In August 1978 there were 635 members of the House of Commons. How many of these were woman?

(a) 25   (b) 50   (c) 100

3 In August 1978 there were 99 members holding ministerial office. How many of them do you think were women?

(a) 5   (b) 25   (c) 50

4 True or false?   There are no female Lords of Appeal or Lord Justices of Appeal.

5.2 Employment

5 True or false?   Women comprise over one third of the labour force.

6 What proportion of married women work:

(a) 20 per cent   (b) 30 per cent   (c) 50 per cent?

7 True or false?   Over 50 per cent of all female non-manual workers work in clerical occupations.

*Some of the following questions are taken from M. Fitzgerald *et al.* (1982) *Know your own society*, Pan Books.

8   Which of the following statements is true? A woman worker with GCE A-levels is likely to earn:

(a) more than   (b) roughly the same   (c) less than

a man with no qualifications?

9   5.3 per cent of men work part-time. What proportion of women work part-time?

10   True or false?
Women comprise less than ten per cent of each of the following professions:

(a) bank managers   (b) chartered accountants   (c) solicitors
(d) architects   (e) consultants   (f) university professors

11   Between 1974 and 1981 male unemployment increased by 300 per cent; by how much did female unemployment increase during the same period?

(a) 100 per cent   (b) 300 per cent   (c) 800 per cent

5.3   Education

12   60 per cent of students gaining O-level pass in Biology are girls. What proportion of those passing O-level Physics are girls?

(a) 15 per cent   (b) 25 per cent   (c) 45 per cent

13   For every 100 boys passing O-level in Technical Drawing, how many girls are there?

(a) less than 5   (b) 15   (c) 40

14   True or false? A girl attending a mixed school is more likely to take Science A-levels (Physics, Chemistry and Mathematics) than a girl attending a single sex school.

15   True or false?   The majority of school teachers are male.

16   True or false?   The majority of head teachers are male.

17   The proportion of full-time women to men students at UK universities is:

(a) one woman to five men   (b) two women to five men
(c) three women to five men

5.4   Marriage, family and the household

18   What is the average life expectancy of a girl born in the 1970s?

(a) 70 years   (b) 76 years   (c) 80 years

19   What age is a woman most likely to be on her wedding day?

(a) under 18   (b) over 18 and under 21   (c) 21-24   (d) 25-29

20   What proportion of the female population marries at least once?

(a) 60 per cent   (b) 75 per cent   (c) over 90 per cent

21   What is the most common number of children in a family nowadays?

22   What proportion of families with dependent children are single parent families?

(a) 5 per cent   (b) 10 per cent   (c) 25 per cent

23   What proportions of children in the UK are born to parents who are not married to each other:

(a) 1 in 5   (b) 1 in 10   (c) 1 in 20

24   Over the years from 1966–1976 has the incidence of divorce

(a) remained the same   (b) doubled   (c) trebled?

25   What is the commonest form of household in the UK?

(a) a married couple   (b) a couple with their children
(c) an individual living alone

5.5 A note about official statistics

The statistics from which we have taken our questions and answers are all published by the Government. If you go to a reasonably sized public library, you will probably find there some of the more common digests of statistics which the Government produces (for example, *Social Trends*, or the *Annual Abstract of Statistics*).

Many people have deeply rooted prejudices about statistics. Some people think there are 'lies, damned lies and statistics', as the saying goes, whereas others treat statistics as simple truths. In effect they are neither. Statistics can be useful as a source of evidence about the different situations of women and men, but they have some quite serious deficiencies. The defects stem from the fact that the Government collects statistics in order to assist it in its tasks of planning and administration, and from the fact that statistics embody assumptions which obscure particular bits of information and render some people, particularly women, almost invisible.

Two key assumptions run through many government statistics. The first is that the household is the basic unit of society, and what goes on in the household is of no concern to policymakers. You may have noticed as you worked through the questions on marriage, family and household or on employment that there weren't any questions about how housework is distributed between the members of the household. This is because the Government does not collect statistics on such questions, because it presumes these to be matters of private concern to the family, and of no interest to policymakers.

The second assumption, which is very evident in statistics on employment and unemployment, is that work is organized according to a masculine norm in which people work full-time from when they leave school or further education or training until they retire, when they stop working. The statistics are notoriously inadequate at recognizing forms of work which do not fit into this prevailing conception of work.

If you are interested in these criticisms of official statistics and want to read further about the deficiencies of the statistics which the Government collects, you might find it interesting to read the article by Paul Allin and Audrey Hunt, 'Women in Official Statistics', in the Course Reader when you have finished the Unit.

Like the other kinds of subject matter we have looked at so far in this Unit — autobiographical writings, newspaper accounts and advertisements — government statistics are socially constructed. This means that the picture of women's situation that emerges from them is selective and constructed. Statistics are, nevertheless, an important means of documenting the situation of women and of comparing women's situation to men's on a number of dimensions. We hope that in working through this Section you have remembered things you had forgotten, and perhaps learned a bit more about the situation of women in contemporary Britain and about inequalities between the sexes.

In Section 6 we shift emphasis again, and look at some of the different kinds of explanation that have been proposed to account for the position of women in contemporary British society.

5.6 Answers to the quiz

1 (a). Between 1951 and 1979 the number of women standing for Parliament rose from 77 to 212. However, the number of women elected as MPs remained virtually unchanged. There were seventeen women MPs in 1951 and nineteen in 1979. (SOURCE *Equal Opportunities Commission (EOC) Research Bulletin*, Vol.1, No.1 1978–9.)

2 (a). In August 1978 the number of women MPs was 27. All the members representing constituencies in Wales and Northern Ireland were men. Proportionately, Scotland had the highest female representation with four women members. (SOURCE *EOC Research Bulletin* Vol.1, No.1, 1978-9.)

3 (a). In 1978 only six out of 99 members holding ministerial office were women. (SOURCE *EOC Research Bulletin*, Vol.1, No.1, 1978–9.)

4 True. In 1977 there were nine Lords of Appeal and sixteen Lord Justices of Appeal, all of whom were men. (SOURCE *EOC Research Bulletin*, Vol.1, No.1, 1978–9.)

5   True. In 1978 women constituted 39.4 per cent of the total labour force.   (SOURCE *EOC Annual Report,* 1980, p.60.)

6   (c). In 1979 51.3 per cent of married women were engaged in paid employment. (SOURCE   *EOC Annual Report,* 1980, p.60.)

7   True. In 1980 54.5 per cent of all female non-manual workers work in clerical and related occupations.   (SOURCE   *EOC Annual Report,* 1980, p.64.)

8   (c). A woman worker with GCE A-levels earns on average less than a man with no qualification. (SOURCE   *General Household Survey,* 1980, Table 6.9, p.115.)

9   40.1 per cent of female employees worked part-time in 1978−9.   (SOURCE   *EOC Research Bulletin,* Vol.1, No.1, 1978−9.)

10   True. Women comprised less than 10 per cent of all these professions in 1977. (SOURCE   *EOC Research Bulletin,* Vol.1, No.1, 1978-9.)

11   (c) 800 per cent. In 1974 male unemployment was 503 300 and female unemployment was 92 400. In September 1981 male unemployment was 2 025 800 and female unemployment 859 000. (SOURCE *Department of Employment Gazette,* 1981.)

12   (b). 23.4 per cent of those passing O-level Physics in England and Wales were female. (SOURCE   *EOC Annual Report,* 1980, p.49.)

13   (a) less than 5. For every 100 boys passing O-level in Technical Drawing in England and Wales in 1978 there were 2.2 girls. (*EOC Annual Report,* 1980, p.49.)

14   False. A girl in a single-sex school in 1975 was more likely to take Science A-levels than a girl in a mixed school. (SOURCE   Department of Education and Science (DES) *Curricular Difference for Boys and Girls, Education Survey 21,* 1975, p.15, Table 2.)

15   The statement is true of secondary school teachers, 56.1 per cent of whom were male in England and Wales in 1978, but not true of primary school teachers, 76.9 per cent of whom were female. (SOURCE   DES, *Statistics of Education, Vol.4 Teachers, 1978,* Table 12.)

16   True. 56.7 per cent of primary school heads in England and Wales in 1978 were male, and 83.3 per cent of secondary school heads were male. (SOURCE   DES *Stattistics of Education. Vol.4 Teachers, 1978,* Table 12.)

17   (b). Women comprised 35.4 per cent of all full-time students at British Universities in 1978. (SOURCE   Calculated from DES *Statistics of Education, Vol.6 Universities 1970−78,* Table 1.)

18   (b). The average life expectancy for a girl born in 1977 is 76.0 years; for a boy it is 69.9 years. (SOURCE   *Social Trends 11,* 1981, Table 8.1)

19   (b). A woman is most likely to be between 18 and 21 years of age when she marries; a man is most likely to be between 21 and 24 years of age. (SOURCE   *Facts in Focus,* Table 7, p.25.)

20   (c). 91.8 per cent of women and 83.5 per cent of men born between 1 January 1944 and 31 January 1945 had married by the time they were 30. The figure rises to well over 90 per cent of both women and men during their life time as a whole: (SOURCE   *Population Trends,* Spring 1979, p.5.)

21   Two. In 1979, 38 per cent of married couples with dependent children had one child, 42 per cent had two children, 15 per cent had three children, and only 4 per cent had four or more children. (SOURCE   *Social Trends 11* 1981, Table 2.6)

22   (b). General Household Survey data suggested that by 1976 one-parent families constituted 11 per cent of families with dependent children, compared with 8 per cent in 1971.   (SOURCE   *EOC Research Bulletin,* Vol.1, No.1, 1978−9.)

23   (b) 1 in 10. Illegitimate babies, as a proportion of all births, has risen from 6 per cent in 1961 to 11 per cent in 1979.   (SOURCE   *Social Trends II,* 1981, Table 2.16.)

24   (c). In the UK in 1966 there were 42 000 decrees nisi. By 1976 the figure had risen to 136 000. (SOURCE   *Social Trends 10,* 1980, Table 2.11.)

25 (b). In 1980, 40 per cent of people lived in households consisting of married couples and their children, 27 per cent in households consisting of married couples alone, 22 per cent were living alone, and 8 per cent were in single-parent households. Only 2 per cent were in households consisting of two or more unrelated persons. (SOURCE *Social Trends 12,* 1982, Table 2.2.)

6 Explanations of gender differences and inequalities

Our aim in this Section is to look at some of the explanations which have been proposed to explain gender differences. We examine three kinds of explanations:

(a) Biologically determinist explanations, which assert that gender differences are determined by the differences in reproductive functions between the sexes.

(b) Explanations which assert that the social situation of women, and inequalities between women and men, are the result of individual acts of prejudice and discrimination.

(c) Explanations which assert that women are oppressed as a group, and that the causes of women's oppression lie in the basic structure of society. We also look at several different variants of this kind of explanation.

These are not the only explanations of gender differences which exist, but they are explanations that you will encounter most frequently during the rest of the Course. This is why we have selected them.

When you read about the different approaches, we want you to think critically about each of them. In particular we want you to think about the differences between the approaches, the advantages and disadvantages of adopting the different perspectives, and the implications of adopting each.

Many of the ideas we discuss also exist in commonsense discourse. We hope that by reading and thinking about these different theoretical arguments you will not only get a feel for different kinds of explanation, but you will also begin to recognize ways in which different explanations permeate everyday thinking about gender differences and inequalities.

●As you read through the following Sections you should try and think about the following questions

1 How does the theory account for differences between women and men?

2 What does the theory say about inequalities between women and men?

3 What relationship does the theory postulate between gender differences and inequalities between women and men?

4 What are the implications of the theory for the possibilities for changing the position of women?

6.1 Biologically determinist explanations

Biologically determinist explanations of sexual difference have a long history in scientific and pre-scientific thinking. They have also had a considerable influence on everyday thinking about the place of women in society. The form of biological arguments has changed over the years. In this Section we look briefly at contemporary arguments which emphasize the role of genes and hormones in determining the development of females and males, and which assert that the situation of women and men is determined by these biological processes. Since these arguments are examined in much more detail by Lynda Birke in Units 2 and 3 we deal with them quite briefly here.

Contemporary proponents of biological determinist explanations assert that the differences between women and men are determined by the differences in reproductive functions between the sexes. There is considerable disagreement about the precise effects of these reproductive differences between the sexes on the subsequent development of women and men. Some people argue that a whole array of differences between women and men — for instance, physiological differences, psychological differences and differences in gender — are based upon reproductive differences between the sexes, whereas others argue that biological factors have only a limited effect on gender differentiation. Let us look a little more closely at the first approach by considering some of the arguments put forward by Mia Kellmer Pringle, who was until recently the Director of the National Children's Bureau:

> The promotion of equal rights and opportunities for women has during recent years gained increasing support, reflected in new laws and regulations. Yet in practice relatively little has changed in the actual position or influence of women. This is similar to the fact that though women obtained the right to vote fifty years ago, their full emancipation did not make much headway during this period. Clearly, laws by themselves are not sufficient. Neither is it primarily a question of treating women as an underprivileged 'minority' for whom special measures are required: nor is the ideal of equality appropriate if this implies as it does for some — that women must become more like men in their aspirations, values behaviour and attitudes.
>
> So far the principle gain has been the opportunity to participate either for the first time or to a greater extent – in areas of life traditionally reserved for men. But surely this is not enough and it does not touch the basic question. This is that equality does not necessarily mean 'sameness'. The central issue is now the role and relationships of both sexes will have to change if women are to be enabled to take their place in society in their own way and in accordance with their own values . . .
>
> These misconceptions spring from the assertion that there are no inherent differences between the sexes and those that appear to exist are due solely to early 'sex typing', historical and traditional accidents and, above all, male chauvinism. And that having equal opportunities means having exactly the same opportunities adopting the same life-style, the same attitudes, characteristics, tastes and interests, and even the same clothes and hair styles.
>
> But surely no one would deny that there is a whole range of physical and physiological differences? Women's height, weight, strength, shape, general appearance and hormonal balance are evidently very different from men's. Therefore is it not also likely that there are temperamental differences? What is unjustifiable and misconceived is the belief that because women are different, therefore they are inferior. (pp.4–5)

Mia Kellmer Pringle goes on to assert that it is women who have been adversely affected by the positive value which society places upon masculine characteristics and the consequent devaluation of feminine characteristics:

> The fact that masculine characteristics are considered superior is surely a reflection of the distorted values of our immature, acquisitive and materialistic society? Why should being self-assertive, aggressive, competitive, status-seeking and thrusting be preferable to being caring, compassionate, tolerant, sensitive and reflective — generally thought to be feminine attributes? Indeed, they are quite essential for the survival of the human race, and it may well be that because only women can conceive and bear children, they have developed a greater capacity for nurturing and caring which has then been further enhanced by the traditional division of labour between the sexes. (p.5)

She lists three harmful effects of this positive valuation of masculine characteristics for women. First, 'liberated' women tend to ape the less likeable characteristics of men, like intellectual prowess, drive and ambition. Second, women tend to be subjected to the pressure of being expected to marry and have children but are made to feel that they are wasting their education or remaining unfulfilled if they choose to devote themselves to their children's care. Third, because caring for children has become undervalued, 'many a mother is being deprived of the sense of achievement and recognition, as well as of joy, which ought to be her due for undertaking the most skilled, demanding and responsible job of all' (p.6).

● Stop for a moment and think about Pringle's arguments. Do you find them satisfactory as an explanation of differences between women and men? Can you find any weak points in her arguments? And can you suggest any counter arguments?

Mia Kellmer Pringle's arguments can be summarized in the form of three propositions. First, there are the sex differences between women and men — e.g. height, weight, strength, shape, general appearance and hormonal balance. Second, there are also temperamental differences between women and men. These, she believes, are also determined by biological factors, although you may have noticed that she establishes this by analogy rather than by logical argument, when she says *'therefore is it not also likely that there are temperamental differences'.* Her third proposition is that these differences do not necessarily constitute inequalities. In the first two paragraphs of the first extract Mia Kellmer Pringle suggest that she is not against trying to attain equal rights for women, so long as equality does not mean that women should become the same as men.

Critics of these kinds of arguments have objected to what they have called their *'biological determinism'*. This is a term which you will find explained in Unit 2 on Biology and the development of sex differences. Briefly, biological determinism can be defined as a theory which claims that physical and physiological characteristics, psychological characteristics and roles can be explained in terms of biological factors, and more specifically in terms of the reproductive differences between males and females.

In general, biologically determinist arguments emphasize the differences between the sexes which they attribute to reproductive differences, and they give these determining weight in explaining psychological characteristics and masculine and feminine gender roles. Different people writing on the subject disagree as to whether they think these differences *necessarily* constitute inequalities, or whether women and men should be considered as being different but equal.

6.2 The liberal view

The second type of explanation we want to look at focuses on the question of inequalities between women and men. It does not deny the existence of biological differences between the sexes but considers these to be inconsequential so far as equality and inequality is concerned. We have called this 'the liberal view', because it accepts the existing structure of society as given but asserts that certain reforms and provisions are necessary for women to attain equality with men and to have freedom of choice about what roles they wish to adopt.

Liberal arguments assume a variety of forms. People who take the view that it is *on account of discrimination* that women seldom reach the top jobs or are under-represented among the population of university students, are adopting a liberal approach to the question of gender inequalities. We decided, in this Section, to concentrate upon the way in which the British Government analyses the situation of women in its sex equality legislation as an example of the liberal view. We therefore focus upon the role of the law in rectifying inequalities. The legal approach is perhaps the dominant form of liberal view in contemporary Britain, but it is not the only form of liberal view. One version of the liberal view is summarized in the following paragraphs taken from the Government White Paper, *Equality for Women*, which provided the basis for the Sex Discrimination Act:

> 16. The unequal status of women has not been perpetuated as the result of the deliberate determination by one half of the population to subject the other half to continued inequality. Its causes are complex and rooted deeply in tradition, custom and prejudice. Beyond the basic physiological differences between men and women lies a whole range of differences between individual men and individual women in all aspects of human ability. The differences within each sex far outweigh the differences between the sexes. But there is insufficient recognition that the variations of character and ability within each sex are greater and more significant than the differences between the sexes. Women are often treated as unequal because they are alleged to be inferior to men in certain respects, and the consequences of their unequal treatment are then seen as evidence of their inferiority. Their unequal status has been caused less by conscious discrimination against women than by the stereotyped attitudes of both sexes about their respective roles. And many who make the important decisions about the treatment of women do not discriminate against them because of conscious personal prejudice but because of prejudices of which they are unaware, or the prejudices (real or assumed) which they ascribe to others—management, employees, customers or colleagues.

> 17. The unequal status of women is wasteful of the potential talents of half our population in a society which, more than ever before, needs to mobilise the skill and ability of all its citizens. Despite the major improvements which have occurred in women's status since the beginning of this century, the pattern of inequality is too pervasive and entrenched to be changed by the gradual process of voluntary initiative. It will not be changed by the mere passage of time. The movement towards equality for women requires the active support and intervention of Government itself. The Government is, therefore, resolved to introduce effective measures to discourage discriminatory conduct and to promote genuine equality of opportunity for both sexes.

● When you have read the extract, stop a minute and try and answer the following questions about the arguments contained within it:

1 How important are biological differences in determining inequalities between women and men?

2 What role have men had in perpetuating inequalities between women and men?

3 What are the causes of inequalities between the sexes?

The White Paper asserts that although there are biological differences between the sexes 'the differences within each sex far outweigh the differences between the sexes'. Thus biological differences are not the only feature in determining gender inequalities. How, then, can these inequalities be explained? The White Paper argues that inequalities do not result from the conscious actions of men: 'the unequal status of women has not been perpetuated as the result of the deliberate determination by one half of the population to subject the other half to continued inequality'. Inequalities, it argues, result from tradition, custom and prejudice. Prejudice results from the traditional and stereotyped attitudes towards women which are held by both men and women, and which are often held unconsciously. Discrimination against women results from these prejudiced attitudes. Thus inequalities between women and men are the product of cumulative acts of discrimination.

Whereas the emphasis of biologically determinist arguments is on the ways in which biological sex differences impose constraints upon the possibilities for changing the position of women and men, the emphasis of the liberal view is on policies that can outlaw discrimination and thereby ameliorate social inequalities. The White Paper focuses upon legal measures which can be used to prevent discrimination. According to the White Paper, the objectives of legislation are:

'to eliminate anti-social practices; to provide remedies for the victim of unfair discrimination; and indirectly to change the prejudiced attitudes expressed as discrimination' (para 20).

The sex equality legislation, which became operative in 1975, was made up of two laws. The Equal Pay Act, which was passed in 1970 and came into force in 1975 (employers having had the intervening five years to move towards equal pay), and the Sex Discrimination Act, passed in 1975.

The Equal Pay Act is concerned, as its title suggests, with women's and men's pay. It applies to basic wage rates and salaries and to all matters that are covered by a contract of employment, like overtime pay, shiftwork allowances, night work premiums, bonuses, luncheon vouchers and other fringe benefits. In order to bring a successful case under the Equal Pay Act, a woman has to prove that she is not being treated equally to a man with respect to any of these benefits. To do this she has to be doing work which is defined as 'like work' with a man — that is, work which is equivalent or broadly similar — so that her work can be compared with his.

The Sex Discrimination Act covers all aspects of employment which are not covered by a contract of employment (for example, recruitment policy, interviewing, hiring, promotion, training, redundancy, etc.), education and provision of goods, facilities and services such as access to housing, mortgages, banks and hire purchase. The Sex Discrimination Act has a more complex definition of discrimination than the Equal Pay Act. It states that:

DISCRIMINATION TO WHICH ACT APPLIES

1.—(1) A person discriminates against a woman in any cir- Sex discrimi-
cumstances relevant for the purposes of any provision of this nation against
Act if— women.

    (a) on the ground of her sex he treats her less favourably than he treats or would treat a man, or

    (b) he applies to her a requirement or condition which he applies or would apply equally to a man but—

        (i) which is such that the proportion of women who can comply with it is considerably smaller than the proportion of men who can comply with it, and

        (ii) which he cannot show to be justifiable irrespective of the sex of the person to whom it is applied, and

        (iii) which is to her detriment because she cannot comply with it.

The discrimination described under (a) is called *direct discrimination*. This means directly discriminating against a woman because of her sex. The discrimination defined under (b) is called *indirect discrimination*. This involves applying a particular test which puts one sex at a disadvantage. One case that went to court in which a woman successfully claimed indirect discrimination found that the Civil Service was discriminating against women because it had a rule that applicants for the Executive Grade should be under the age of 28. A woman called Belinda Price challenged this, claiming that women who had children in their twenties and stayed at home to look after them could not conform to the age requirements and were therefore prevented from entering the Executive Grade. This was held to be an instance of indirect discrimination.

The sex equality legislation and the White Paper on which it is based contain a specific analysis of sexual difference and inequalities between women and men. It shares with biologically determinist arguments the view that some sexual differences are biologically determined, but it regards these as relatively unimportant so far as women's claim to equal rights is concerned. It assumes that there are inequalities between women and men and that these are a result not of biological differences but of tradition, custom and prejudice. More specifically it asserts that inequalities are a result of individual acts of discrimination which have been perpetuated by prejudiced individuals. In the liberal view, the law has a major role to play in rectifying inequalities between women and men.

In the two types of explanation we have considered so far — biologically determinist explanations and liberal explanations — the major issues that have been raised by the different theories are: How can sexual differences be accounted for? What is the relationship between sexual differences and inequalities between women and men? And what accounts for inequalities between women and men, and how can these be ameliorated?

● Before we go on to consider the remaining theories, spend a few minutes writing down how the two different kinds of approach you have read about so far in this Section would answer each of the above questions.

6.3 Analyses of women's oppression

The remaining types of approach that we shall consider are all concerned with women as a social category, or social group, and not with individuals, and they focus upon precisely those institutionalized forms of inequality that the liberal view ignores. Broadly speaking, they all analyse inequalities between women and men as a set of institutionalized relationships in which women as a group are oppressed. Each of the approaches believes that women's oppression is rooted in the basic structure of society. They disagree, however, in their analysis of the causes of women's oppression.

3.1 Women's oppression located in power relations

The first kind of analysis we shall consider grew out of the contemporary feminist movement in the USA. This argues that women as a social group are dominated by men as a social group and that this domination of women by men occurs within a set of institutionalized relationships called patriarchy. To help you understand the basic structure of this argument, which has been extremely influential within feminist thinking over the past ten years, we shall briefly look at some extracts from Kate Millett's book *Sexual Politics*, which was published in the USA in 1970. Millett argues that:

> . . . a disinterested examination of our system of sexual relationships must point out that the situation between the sexes now, and throughout history, is a case of that phenomenon Max Weber defined as *herrschaft*, a relationship of dominance and subordinance. What goes largely unexamined, often even unacknowledged (yet is institutionalized nonetheless) in our social order, is the birthright priority whereby males rule females. Through this system a most ingenious form of "interior colonization" has been achieved. It is one which tends moreover to be sturdier than any form of segregation, and more rigorous than class stratification, more uniform, certainly more enduring. However muted its present appearance may be, sexual dominion obtains nevertheless as perhaps the most pervasive ideology of our culture and provides its most fundamental concept of power.

> This is so because our society, like all other historical civilizations, is a patriarchy. The fact is evident at once if one recalls that the military, industry, technology, universities, science, political office and finance — in short, every avenue of power within the society, including the coercive force of the police, is entirely in male hands. (pp.24–5)

If you are not familiar with contemporary feminist writings you may have encountered a number of unfamiliar terms in this extract, or familiar words which are used in unfamiliar ways. Kate Millett talks about 'internal colonization', which is a term she borrows from the black liberation movement — which existed in the United States (and to a much lesser extent in Britain) before the current wave of feminism — and which refers to the fact that domination not only takes place in the public world but also internally, in people's heads. She also talks about sexual domination as a 'fundamental concept of power,' and argues for giving a new meaning to terms like 'power' and 'politics'.

Kate Millett uses 'politics' to refer to any power-structured relationships, and outlines her own definition of politics in the following terms:

> This essay does not define the political as that relatively narrow and exclusive world of meetings, chairmen and parties. The term "politics" shall refer to power-structured relationships, arrangements whereby one group of persons is controlled by another. (p.23).

Sexual politics, then, refers to power-structured relationships whereby women are controlled by men. Kate Millett gives some idea of what she means by 'power' in the following passage:

> . . . it may be imperative that we give some attention to defining a theory of politics which treats of power relations on grounds less conventional than those to which we are accustomed. I have therefore found it pertinent to define them on grounds of personal contact and interaction between members of well-defined and coherent groups: races, castes, classes, and sexes. For it is precisely because certain groups have no representation in a number of recognized political structures that their position tends to be so stable, their oppression so continuous. (p.24)

You should note that Kate Millett's definitions of *power* and *politics* are much broader than the definition implied in the White Paper on Sex Equality. In her analysis, all kinds of relationships — including interpersonal relationships between men and women — are seen as power relationships, and therefore fall within the realm of politics.

Kate Millett asserts that the power relationships in which men control women are institutionalized within patriarchy. The concept of patriarchy is extremely important in contemporary feminist writings, so it is important that you try and grasp what is meant by it.

● Look back at the extract from Kate Millett on pp.43-4 and try to figure out how she defines patriarchy

---

Kate Millett defines patriarchy as a society in which power resides in male hands. She goes on to state that there are two principles governing patriarchy:

> If one takes patriarchal government to be the institution whereby that half of the populace which is female is controlled by that half which is male, the principles of patriarchy appear to be two fold: male shall dominate female, older male shall dominate younger. (p.25)

Patriarchy can vary from one situation to another:

> While patriarchy as an institution is a social constant so deeply entrenched as to run through all other political, social, or economic forms, whether of caste or class, feudality or bureaucracy, just as it pervades all major religions, it also exhibits great variety in history and locale. (p.25)

In democracies, for instance, she says, women may hold office (i.e. there may be exceptions to the rule that male shall dominate female) but this occurs 'in such miniscule numbers' that they are 'below even token representation' (p.26).

Kate Millett's analysis departs radically from biologically determinist analyses over the question of the role of biological differences in determining gender differences. She states that:

> . . . it must be admitted that many of the generally understood distinctions between the sexes in the more significant areas of role and temperament, not to mention status, have in fact, essentially cultural, rather than biological, bases. Attempts to prove that temperamental dominance is inherent in the male (which for its advocates, would be tantamount to validating logically as well as historically, the patriarchal situation regarding role and status) have been notably unsuccessful. (p.28)

She therefore emphasizes the importance of social, and cultural factors as the foundation of patriarchy; and particularly emphasizes the importance of the family as the cornerstone of patriarchy:

> Patriarchy's chief institution is the family. It is both a mirror of and a connection with the larger society; a patriarchal unit within a patriarchal whole. Mediating between the individual and the social structure, the family effects control and conformity where political and other authorities are insufficient. As the fundamental instrument and the foundation unit of patriarchal society the family and its roles are prototypical. Serving as an agent of the larger society, the family not only encourages its own members to adjust and conform, but acts as a unit in the government of the patriarchal state which rules its citizens through its family heads. Even in patriarchal societies where they are granted legal citizenship, women tend to be ruled through the family alone and have little or no formal relation to the state. (p.33)

This approach has been extremely important in contemporary feminist thinking. Theories like Kate Millett's (which are often called radical feminist theories) have drawn attention to the centuries of power and domination in relationships between women and men, and have suggested that the situation of *all* women is determined by these patriarchal relationships in *all* societies. This kind of analysis has implications for endeavours to change the situation of women which are rather different from the 'equal rights' approach of advocates of the liberal view.

Whereas the liberal view takes the existing structure of society as given, but asserts that certain reforms have to be effected for women to have equality of opportunity within it, the radical feminist view asserts that the oppression of women is firmly entrenched in the very heart of patriarchal institutions, and that the structure of society will have to be changed, and male power eroded, for women to be free.

The task of feminism, according to this view, involves challenging the structures of male power and domination. It involves *women's liberation*. This is different from the role which advocates of the liberal view ascribe to feminism, which can be summed up by the term *women's emancipation*. The major difference between women's liberation and women's emancipation is that emancipation involves changing the position of women within the existing framework of society, whereas women's liberation involves transforming the social framework.

● Spend a few minutes making a note of the similarities and differences between the liberal view and the radical feminist approach as exemplified by Kate Millett's *Sexual Politics*. Think in particular of the ways in which each analyses the causes of inequalities between women and men.

6.3.2. Women's oppression related to the organization of production

The second kind of analysis of women's oppression that we want to consider also asserts that the oppression of women is rooted in the structure of society. Like radical feminism this approach focuses upon the institutionalized forms of inequality which the liberal view ignores. It differs in several important ways, however, in the account it gives of the causes of women's oppression. The approach we want to discuss is often described as a Marxist feminist one. As the term implies, people working within this framework have tried to effect a *rapprochement* between Marxist analysis (so called because Karl Marx laid the foundations for it) and a feminist analysis.

Sheila Rowbotham's book, *Woman's Consciousness, Man's World*, first published in Britain in 1973, is one example of a Marxist feminist approach. To enable you to get some idea of the basic tenets of this approach, we shall consider some extracts from

Sheila Rowbotham's book. The following extracts are about women's oppression within a specifically capitalist form of society like that of contemporary Britain. Marxist feminists argue that although women are oppressed in all societies the form of this oppression and the causes of women's oppression are different in different kinds of society. Thus, for instance, women's oppression takes a different form in feudal societies from the form it takes in capitalist societies.

This is one important difference between a radical feminist perspective like Kate Millett's and a Marxist feminist approach like Sheila Rowbotham's. Whereas radical feminists emphasize the continuity of patriarchy and of male domination and female subordination across different kinds of society, Marxist feminists emphasize the ways in which women's oppression changes historically. They also emphasize the importance of class differences between women within any particular society. The concept of social class and the notion of class differences have a specific meaning within a Marxist feminist perspective, which may be unfamiliar to you. According to this approach social classes refer to categories of people who have different relations to the organization of production*.

In the following extract Sheila Rowbotham is referring to the situation of women within the working class – that is, within the population which has to earn its living; she is not referring to those who own capital or land. She outlines what is meant by the term *the sexual division of labour*:

> the sexual division of labour means that men and women are at different points in the structure of social relationships. Men as a group have a different relation from women as a group to the means of production. Women enter commodity production, and, like men, produce goods which circulate as commodities; they thus share the exploitation and experience of alienation of male workers in capitalism. But, because within the social division of labour in capitalism — the task of maintaining and reproducing commodity producers is largely given to women, the expenditure of female labour power in procreation and in the nourishing of men and children at home determines how much female labour can be expended in the production of commodities. (pp.58–9)

● After you have read the passage stop for a minute and make a note of how, in your own words, you would define the sexual division of labour.

The sexual division of labour refers to the different positions which women and men occupy within the structure of society. It is related to a specialization of roles, or differentiation of functions, between women and men.

● Now make a note of what, according to Rowbotham, are the main tasks within the sexual division of labour performed by women.

Sheila Rowbotham talks about two kinds of activities that are generally performed by women within the family — child-bearing and child-rearing, and housework. People generally think of giving birth to and looking after children (particularly young children) as activities which women are 'naturally' suited to, and housework is often talked about as a 'labour of love', which women perform for those whom they love. Sheila Rowbotham suggests in the above extract that these activities are essential to the operation of the economy. Her argument can be summarized as follows.

Bearing and raising children is essential because children will be the next generation of workers when they grow up. And housework is an integral part of the operation of the economy because workers have to be fed, clothed and looked after. Sheila Rowbotham therefore suggests that, despite the fact that the family is normally thought of as an essentially 'private' world, in which people are free to engage in their personal lives and relationships without economic pressures and state interference, it is an integral part of the capitalist economy. Similarly, she argues, women's activities within the family are essential for the organization of production to carry on.

---

*Different Unit authors define the concept of social class in slightly different ways: sometimes in relation to production, sometimes in relation to occupation, and sometimes in relation to life style. We hope the definition we give here will help you begin to work with the term.

We want to draw your attention to two other terms which Sheila Rowbotham uses in the above passage. The first of these is *production*. Broadly speaking the term production refers to the means used to appropriate and gain control over nature. You might find it useful to think of production as being like the economy. You should remember, however, that Marxist feminists tend to define the term production very broadly. You should remember, too, that in a Marxist feminist framework the organization of production, or the economy is conceptualized as a social process, and Marxist feminists assume that the form of organization of the economy can be changed.

The second term which we want to draw to your attention is *reproduction*. In common-sense discourse the term reproduction normally refers to the process of reproducing the species. Lynda Birke discusses in Units 2 and 3 whether or not the process of reproduction can be understood solely as a biological process which is independent of social factors; and you will find further discussion of the processes of reproduction in the family and the state in other Units. For the moment we wish to point out that Sheila Rowbotham is using the term reproduction to refer both to child-bearing (reproduction of the species) and to caring for children and housework. The term, therefore, has a broader meaning as Sheila Rowbotham uses it than it has in common usage.

In another passage from the same chapter Sheila Rowbotham suggests that one consequence of the sexual division of labour is that women and men experience the worlds of work and the family differently:

> Men and women are brought up for a different position in the labour force: the man for the world of work, the woman for the family. This difference in the sexual division of labour in society means that the relationship of men as a group to production is different from that of women. For a man the social relations and values of commodity production predominate and home is a retreat into intimacy. For the woman the public world belongs to and is owned by men. She is dependent on what the man earns but is responsible for the private sphere, the family. In the family she does a different kind of work from the man . . . The social relationships in the family . . . are different from those outside, although they hinge on commodity production. Thus these differences in the way in which production is structured serve to shape the consciousness of men and women. In the case of women who go out to work, the main responsibility is still the home. (pp.61–2)

How is the existence of the sexual division of labour in capitalist societies to be explained, according to this perspective? Some people have argued that the explanation for the sexual division of labour lies in the 'needs' of the capitalist mode of production (e.g for the tasks of reproduction to be carried out without cost within the family, or for a cheap and flexible labour force). Others have argued that this is a rather circular kind of explanation, and have suggested that the explanation lies in a variety of factors: in the fact that capitalist society developed out of feudal society, in which there were gender divisions and inequalities between the sexes; in the development of the capitalist mode of production, which led to the separation of the workplace from the household, and the removal of wage labour from the home; in the role of men (as employers, trade unionists and husbands), who made sure that it was women who continued to perform the role of housewife; in the continuing requirement in a society based upon profitability that the costs of labour and the costs of reproducing the working population are kept low; and in the prevalence of familial ideology within the capitalist mode of production that decrees that a woman's place is in the home.

The final term we want to introduce you to which is important in Marxist feminist analysis is the term *ideology*.

● If you look back at the extract from Micheline Wandor on p.15 you will see that she describes how her rationale for having children fitted sweetly into the *dominant ideology*. Can you guess, from Micheline Wandor's use of the term *dominant ideology* and from our comments about *familial ideology* in the last paragraph, what the term ideology means? Make a few notes on this.

Ideology refers to clusters of ideas, beliefs and attitudes. The *dominant ideology* refers to the prevailing ideas, beliefs and attitudes within society. Yet, an ideology is not simply a set of ideas that exists in abstraction from society; it defines, shapes and explains the social world and people's position within it. Many ideologies contain accounts of what are the appropriate roles and forms of behaviour for men and women. One of the characteristics of an ideology is that it offers a partial explanation of the social world and of people's positions within it. Ideologies which are concerned with gender divisions frequently assert that the sexual division of labour is natural and universal, thereby implying that it cannot be changed. In analysing the role of ideology in constructing gender differences, feminists have tried to point out the ways in which dominant ideological interpretations provide a partial and distorted explanation of the sexual division of labour by asserting that it is natural and universal rather than historical and social.

Classical Marxism argues that the position of the dominated classes within class societies can only be changed by fundamentally changing the structure of production within the society and the form of all social institutions and social relationships which are based upon this system of production. The Marxist emphasis upon the importance of socialist transformation of society stems from the view that social inequalities cannot be overcome until the system of production which gives rise to the existence of social classes is transcended. Marxist feminists argue that women's oppression is closely tied up with the oppression of social classes within any society. Marxist feminists share with radical feminists a belief that the situation of women can only be transformed through women's liberation. They also assert – and this makes them different from the other feminists approaches that we have discussed in this Unit – that some kind of socialist transformation is necessary for women's oppression to be ended (although few Marxist feminists presume that the oppression of women is automatically ended by socialist transformation).

● You may have found this Section on Marxist feminism quite difficult to understand. In order to test your understanding, and to help you think about the differences and similarities between the theories we have discussed, spend a few minutes making a few notes about how you think Marxist feminist theory would answer the questions we posed at the beginning of Section 6:

(a) How can sexual differences be accounted for?

(b) What is the relationship between sexual differences and inequalities between women and men?

(c) What accounts for inequalities between women and men, and how can these be ameliorated?

6.3.3 Women's oppression rooted in biological differences

Most contemporary feminist analyses adopt a strongly critical stance towards biologically determinist theories. Some feminists, however, use arguments which are closely akin to biologically determinist theories in analysing women's oppression. Lynda Birke discusses some of these arguments in Unit 3. For the moment we shall concentrate upon one such approach, exemplified by Shulamith Firestone's book, *The Dialectics of Sex*. Like Kate Millett's *Sexual Politics* this was also published in the USA in 1970. Shulamith Firestone's arguments might seem rather outlandish to those of you who are new to them. We have included them because *The Dialectic of Sex* — like *Sexual Politics* and *Woman's Consciousness, Man's World* — is somewhat of a classic among contemporary feminist writings and because we think Shulamith Firestone raises interesting questions for you to think about. She writes:

... let us first try to develop an analysis in which biology itself — procreation — is at the origin of the dualism*. The immediate assumption of the layman that the unequal division of the sexes is 'natural' may be well-founded. We need not immediately look beyond this. Unlike economic class, sex class sprang directly from a biological reality: men and women were created different, and not equal. Although, as De Beauvoir points out, this difference of itself did not necessitate the development of a class system — the domination of one group by another — the reproductive *functions* of these differences did. The biological family is an inherently unequal power distribution. The need for power leading to the development of classes arises from the psychosexual formation of each individual according to the basic imbalance... (p.16)

● After reading this extract stop for a minute and compare Shulamith Firestone's arguments with Kate Millett's. What are the similarities and differences between the two approaches?

You might have noticed that both writers emphasize the domination of women by men. Both also emphasize the unequal power relationships within the family. For Shulamith Firestone, however, these unequal power relationships are rooted in the reproductive difference between men and women. It is men's need to control women's reproductive capacity which has led men to dominate women. You should note that she uses the term 'sex classes' to refer to men and women. These are similar to the social classes which exist within the Marxist feminist framework in that both imply unequal relationships between two groups of people. Unlike social classes, however, sex classes are, according to Firestone, rooted in biological differences.

You may be wondering whether this makes Shulamith Firestone a biological determinist, since, like Mia Kellmer Pringle, she asserts that gender differences between women and men are rooted in biological differences between the sexes. It is difficult to give a precise answer to this question. In many ways, Shulamith Firestone is a biological determinist because she explains gender differences between women and men in terms of reproductive differences between the sexes. In other respects, her analysis is radically different from conventional biologically determinist theories like Mia Kellmer Pringle's. For a start, she asserts that the relationships between women and men are fundamentally relations of power. Furthermore, unlike Mia Kellmer Pringle, Shulamith Firestone argues that it is possible to transform the relationships by which men dominate women, as is evident from the following extract

The problem becomes political, demanding more than a comprehensive historical analysis, when one realizes that though man is increasingly capable of freeing himself from the biological conditions that created his tyranny over women and children, he has little reason to want to give this tyranny up ...

Though the sex class system may have originated in fundamental biological conditions, this does not guarantee once the biological basis of their oppression has been swept away that women and children will be freed. On the contrary, the new technology, especially fertility control, may be used against them to reinforce the entrenched system of exploitation.

*The dualism which Shulamith Firestone refers to is the dualism between man and woman. In this passage she is criticizing Simone de Beauvoir's analysis in *The Second Sex*.

So that just as to assure elimination of economic classes requires the revolt of the underclass (the proletariat) and, in a temporary dictatorship, their seizure of the means of *production,* so to assure the elimination of sexual classes requires the revolt of the underclass (women) and the seizure of control of *reproduction:* not only the full restoration to women of ownership of their own bodies, but also their (temporary) seizure of control of human fertility — the new population biology as well as all the social institutions of child-bearing and child-rearing. And just as the end goal of socialist revolution was not only the elimination of the economic class *privilege* but of the economic class *distinction* itself, so the end goal of feminist revolution must be, unlike that of the first feminist movement, not just the elimination of male *privilege* but of sex *distinction* itself: genital differences between human beings would no longer matter culturally . . . The reproduction of the species by one sex for the benefit of both would be replaced by (at least the option of) artificial reproduction: children would be born to both sexes equally, or independently of either, however one chooses to look at it; the dependence of the child on the mother (and vice versa) would give way to a greatly shortened dependence on a small group of others in general, and any remaining inferiority to adults in physical strength would be compensated for culturally. The division of labour would be ended by the elimination of labour altogether (through cybernetics). The tyranny of the biological family would be broken.

And with it the psychology of power . . .   (pp.18—19)

• Look back at the extract and make a note of what, in Shulamith Firestone's view, would need to be changed for women to be freed from male domination.

· Shulamith Firestone argues that women need to seize control of *reproduction,* of their own fertility. Eventually, she asserts, the goal of a feminist revolution is the elimination of the sex distinction itself through removing the reproduction of the species from women. Only then, according to her, would the power of the biological family be broken. Like Kate Millett and like Sheila Rowbotham, Shulamith Firestone emphasizes the importance of women's liberation. In her view the aim of women's liberation is to eliminate the sex distinction itself. According to her, only when the role of women in reproducing the species is removed, will the sexual division of labour be eroded.

6.4 The theories compared

The theories which we have dealt with in Section 6 differ in a number of respects.

• Stop and think for a moment about how you think the theories differ, and make a note of any differences which occur to you.

There are a whole array of differences between the theories which you might have picked out. We want to pinpoint three differences which strike us as being particularly important.

The theories differ in the extent to which they emphasize the role of biological sex differences in the determination of gender differences. The first set of theories we looked at, biologically determinist theories, gives considerable weight to biological sex differences, and holds these responsible for the different social positions of women and men. Shulamith Firestone also emphasizes biological sex differences. The other theories we have considered vary in the weight they give to biological sex differences. The liberal view, and Marxist feminist theory, for instance, do not deny the existence of biological sex differences. They do, however, argue that these have a limited role in determining the social positions of women and men. They place their main emphasis upon social and economic factors in determining the postion of women. Kate Millett's is perhaps the extreme case of an anti-biologically reductionist theory, so much so that she is sometimes critized for sociological reductionism (i.e. explaining gender differences entirely in social terms without regard to biological factors).

The theories also differ as to whether they think that the unequal position of women results from the act of individuals (e.g. prejudice and discrimination), as the liberal view proposes, or whether they think inequalities between women and men are rooted in the structure of society more generally. Kate Millett, Shulamith Firestone and Sheila Rowbotham all share the belief that women's oppression is rooted in the structure of society more generally. However, each provides a rather different account of what they think it is about the structure of society that gives rise to women's oppression and to inequalities between the sexes.

Radical feminism places its main emphasis upon the power relationships by which men dominate women which, it argues, are institutionalized within patriarchy. Shulamith Firestone, too, emphasizes male power over women, but argues that the foundations of this power lie in men's control over women's reproductive capacities.

Marxist feminism places much more emphasis upon economic relationships, and particularly upon the ways in which the organization of production gives rise to different kinds of relationships between the sexes.

Finally the theories have rather different implications for social change. The liberal approach places considerable emphasis upon the law and changing people's attitudes in order to erode inequalities between the sexes. It focuses upon women's emancipation, that is, change within the existing framework of society. The three feminist approaches that we have discussed in the Section 6.3 argue that a more radical transformation of existing social relationships is necessary in order to erode inequalities between the sexes. They focus upon the liberation of women.

In practice the differences between the theories are less stark than we have portrayed them here. You will find as you read through the rest of the Course that many Unit authors make common assumptions and use similar concepts (e.g. the concept of patriarchy) even though they may work with different theoretical perspectives. There are many common assumptions because people who are involved in concretely analysing the position of women in a given period (for example, the early nineteenth century) or in a particular sphere (for instance, paid work, or health care) have come to appreciate that the position of women, and relationships between the sexes, are structured in quite complex ways. They have also become increasingly aware of the importance of a variety of determining factors — biological factors, power relations between women and men, ideology, and the organization of production — rather than a single determining cause of women's oppression.

They wouldn't use them long words if they had to clean up after themselves!

⚡ Conclusion

We have analysed the situation of women in a number of different ways in this Unit. We started off by considering the question of women's experience. In Section 2 we looked at a series of autobiographical extracts, because we wanted you to think about whether, and in what ways, women share a set of common experiences as women. In Section 3 we asked you to think about women's experience in rather a different way — by looking at how women are represented in newspapers. Section 4 was again concerned with how women are represented, this time visually, through ads. At the end of Section 4 we suggested that representations of women's experiences are always constructed — even where women appear to be writing or speaking about themselves in very different ways, as in autobiographies. In Section 5 we asked you to think about selected aspects of the situation of women in contemporary Britain by doing a quiz based upon official statistics. We also suggested that even statistical evidence is constructed, and that this gives you a partial view of women's situation. Section 6 turned to the difficult question of explanations. We looked at a variety of explanations of gender differences and inequalities between the sexes. First we looked at biologically determinist theories which assert that gender differences and inequalities between women and men are determined by reproductive differences between the sexes. Next we looked at the liberal view, which suggests that biological sex differences are of little importance in determining inequalities between the sexes, and which asserts that inequalities stem from individual acts of prejudice and discrimination. We then examined three different kinds of theory which argue that the situation of women, and inequalities between the sexes, are rooted in the basic structure of society . . . The first approach (exemplified by Kate Millett's *Sexual Politics*) emphasized the power relations between women and men. The second, Marxist feminist, approach (exemplified by Sheila Rowbotham's *Woman's Consciousness, Man's World)* suggested that inequalities between the sexes are related to the form of organization of production. The third approach (exemplified by Shulamith Firestone's *The Dialectic of Sex)* argued that men's power over women is rooted in their control of women's reproductive capacities. We do not expect you to be able to remember all the different arguments that we have discussed in this Introductory Unit. We hope, however, that it has opened up for you some of the ideas which will be developed in much more detail throughout the Course, and that you will have found it useful as a starting point for thinking about how, and why, women's experience is changing.

Now that you have worked through this Unit we hope that you have gained:

1   An appreciation of the importance of autobiographical accounts in understanding the experience of women.   (Section 2)

2   An ability to be critical of the ways in which women are written about in the press, and how these differ from the ways in which men are written about.   (Section 3)

3   An ability to be critical of the ways in which women are represented visually in the media, especially in advertisements.   (Section 4)

4   An understanding of what the *social construction of women's experience* means. (Sections 2, 3 and 4)

5   An appreciation that the ways in which official statistics are classified embodies assumptions about women and men.   (Section 5)

6   An outline of the structure of biologically determinist explanations, liberal explanations, and feminist explanations, and an understanding of how these differ from each other.   (Section 6)

7   Some understanding of what is meant by the following concepts: sex and gender, patriarchy, discrimination, the sexual division of labour, social class, production, reproduction, ideology.

References and further reading

ALLEN P. and HUNT, A. (1982) Women in Official Statistics, *The Changing Experience of Women,* Martin Robertson.

BEAUVOIR, S. DE (1972) *The Second Sex*, Penguin.

COOTE, A. and CAMPBELL, B. (1982) *Sweet Freedom,* Pan Books.

DAVIES, M. LLEWELYN (1977) *Life as We Have Known it,* Virago.

DOWRICK, S. and GRUNDBERG, S. (1980) *Why Children?* The Women's Press.

FIRESTONE, S. (1979) *The Dialectic of Sex,* The Women's Press.

FITZGERALD, M. *et al.* (1982) *Know Your Own Society,* Pan Books.

HMSO (1974) *Equality for Women,* Cmd 5724.

HOBBES, M. (1973) *Born to Struggle,* Quartet Books.

KING, J. and STOTT, M. (eds) (1972) *Is this you Life? Images of Women in the Media,* Virago.

MILLETT, K. (1970) *Sexual Politics,* Doubleday.

MITCHELL, J. (1976) *Woman's Estate*, Penguin.

POLLOCK, G. (Autumn 1977) What's Wrong with Images of Women? *Screen Education No. 24*.

PRINGLE, M. KELLMER *et al.* (1980) *A Fairer Future for Children*, Macmillan.

ROWBOTHAM, S. (1973) *Women's Consciousness, Man's World*, Penguin.

ROWBOTHAM, S. (1973) *Hidden from History*, Pluto Press.

SPENCE, J. (1978–9) What do People do all Day? Class and Gender Images of Women, *Screen Education No. 29*.

WILSON, A. (1976) *Finding a Voice*, Virago.

WILSON, E. (1982) *Mirror Writing*, Virago.

WILLIAMSON, J. (1978) *Decoding Advertisements, Ideology and Meaning in Advertising*, Marion Boyars.

WOOLF, V. (ed, Jeanne Schulkind) (1976) *Moments of Being*, The University Press, Sussex.

Note Any of the above items would make interesting further reading.

Acknowledgements

Grateful acknowledgement is made to the following sources for permission to reproduce material in this unit:

Text

Llewelyn Davies, M. (1977) *Life As We Have Known It*, Virago, reprinted by permission of the Author's Literary Estate and The Hogarth Press; Woolf, V. (1976) *Moments of Being*, ed. J. Schulkind, Sussex University Press/Chatto and Windus, reprinted by permission of the Author's Estate, The Hogarth Press and Harcourt Brace Jovanovich Inc., New York. Hobbes, M. (1973) *Born to Struggle*, Quartet Books; Wandor, M. (1980) *Why Children?* eds S. Dowrick and S. Grundberg, The Women's Press; Tandon, Dr K. (1983) 'Lumps and bumps, racism and sexism', *Spare Rib*, 135, October; Coote, A. and Campbell, B. (1982) *Sweet Freedom*, Basil Blackwell Ltd; Firestone, S. (1979) *The Dialectic of Sex*, The Women's Press.

Figures

Figure 1 courtesy of Brabantia (UK) Ltd; *Figure 2* courtesy of Ogilvy and Mather Ltd; *Figure 3* courtesy of Pioneer Electronic (Europe) N. V.; *Figure 4* courtesy of Halifax Building Society; *Figure 5* courtesy of The Boots Company Ltd; *Figure 6* courtesy of Carreras Rothmans Ltd; *Figure 7* courtesy of Robinson and Sons Ltd; *Figure 8* Jill Posener; Figure 9 'Buy some apples, Buy some bananas' © 1972 ARTnews Annual from *Woman As Sex Object*; *Figure 10 (left)* Bayer (UK) Ltd; Figure 10 (right) Avril Ravenscroft.

Illustrations

p. 11 Quentin Bell; p. 18 Andrew Yeadon; *pp. 23 and 24* Associated Newspapers Ltd; *p. 26* Liz Mackie from Thompson, J. (compiler) (1980) *Equality for some: a tape-study pack for women*, National Extension College, Cambridge; *p. 35 The Guardian*, 9 December, 1981; *pp. 40 and 51* Liz Mackie; *p. 41* Lesley Ruda from Thompson, J. (compiler) (1980) *Equality for some: a tape-study pack for women*, National Extension College, Cambridge; *p. 43* Lesley Ruda; *p. 47* See Red Womens Workshop.

Cover

Battered women demand freedom, Liz Heron; De Beers advertisement, Jill Posener; Book cover, reproduced with permission of Virago Press from the cover of *Life as we have known it*, edited by Margaret Llewelyn Davies, Virago, 1977; girl at drilling machine, John Hearn/Equal Opportunities Commission.

U221 The Changing Experience of Women

Unit 1 The woman question

Unit 2 ⎱ Nature and culture
Unit 3 ⎰

Unit 4 Sexuality

Unit 5 Reading women writing

Unit 6 Femininity and women's magazines

Unit 7 Women in the household

Unit 8 Development of family and work

Unit 9 The family

Unit 10 ⎱ Women and employment
Unit 11 ⎰

Unit 12 Economic dependence and the State

Unit 13 Educating girls

Unit 14 Health and medicine

Unit 15 Violence against women

Unit 16 Moving forward